IRAN
Desperate
for God

*An oppressive Islamic state
drives its people
into the arms of Christ*

Living Sacrifice Book Company
Bartlesville, OK

Iran: Desperate for God

Living Sacrifice Book Company
P.O. Box 2273
Bartlesville, OK 74005-2273

ISBN 0-88264-007-0

Design and production by Genesis Group

Cover by David Marty Design

Printed in the United States of America

*Dedicated to our courageous Iranian
brothers and sisters who, for security
reasons, cannot be named*

❧❧

Special thanks to those who helped to
conduct interviews and edit the material
for this book:

Todd Nettleton
Kay Rizzo
Cheryl O.
Georgiana M.
Lynn Copeland
Vanessa F.
Tom White

CONTENTS

॰॰

The Six-Year-Old Evangelist

Tom White

In Tehran, Iran, a six-year-old boy began watching an illegal Christian broadcast about Jesus Christ. As he listened to these followers of Jesus, he memorized their songs, sang along with them, and prayed when they prayed. One morning during breakfast before leaving for school, he said to his mother, "I want to tell my teacher about Jesus. What can I do?" Together they devised a plan. As she walked with him down the street to the school, she prayed for his safety, wondering, *Does God really desire this much obedience or sacrifice from my family?*

The boy entered the excited, noisy classroom and set his heavier-than-usual backpack by his desk. The children all sat down, and the morning lessons began. As students were looking down at their work, he quietly walked up to the teacher's desk with a lesson sheet.

He whispered to the teacher, "Do you want to know about Jesus?"

She nodded her head yes.

"Okay, this is what I will do. When it is time for recess, I will put my backpack by the door, unzip it and leave it open. After all the students leave the class, you go and pick up the Bible and the video from my backpack."

Later in the morning, the children all ran outside to play. The backpack was now near the door. Later, when the sweaty, happy group ran back inside, the boy carried it back to his desk. It wasn't so heavy now.

The next day he asked her, "Did you read the Bible? Did you watch the video? What do you think of Jesus?"

DESPITE THE TREMENDOUS OPPRESSION AND SCARCITY OF BELIEVERS, AN INTENSE SPIRITUAL HUNGER IS BREAKING OUT ACROSS THE NATION.

Across town an elderly man with a white moustache strolls along the sidewalk. The evening air is cooling down, so families are out walking or sitting on blankets by the river. The grandfather stops to look at a baby, pat a head, and visit in the fraternal Iranian way.

After talking awhile to an interested group, he hands out a few booklets, some pamphlets and, at times, a New Testament to the curious, the receptive. The following evening he is out again, but plainclothes police are present this time. They grab his material and beat him, knocking his silver-rimmed spectacles off his face. Taking him over to his car, they find a box of New Testaments in the back seat. Making the situation even worse, he is a Muslim who has become a Christian. The officers take him to jail. Some weeks later, after appeals from relatives and a large "favor," the judge releases him.

A few months pass by. Then on the other side of town, a familiar figure shuffles quietly across a wide pedestrian bridge. There he is again, materials in his bag, a loving word, relaxed conversations about love, God, problems, the meaning of life.

⟨⟩

A six-year-old boy and a grandfather—followers of Jesus Christ in a nation branded as a leading exporter of terrorism. What circumstances have produced such courageous Christians? How can it be that they are so bold—or that they exist at all?

In Iran, ethnic groups that are allowed to practice Christianity, such as the Armenians, compose less than 10 percent of the population. Most believers prefer not to share their faith because of the danger involved. (There have been Christian heroes among Armenian evangelicals. For the past fifteen years, many have been martyred or imprisoned.) Despite the tremendous oppression and scarcity of believers, an intense spiritual hunger is breaking out across the nation.

During my last trip to Iran, my Iranian guide stayed up all night reading the New Testament I had given him. At breakfast, he was overflowing with questions and positive comments about Jesus Christ. He was young, had a family, as well as a degree in English literature. He took me to his home for tea where his gracious wife and children received me with great honor and hospitality.

This family represents the unknown Iran—not the screaming mobs in the street, not the long lines of religious mourners walking along the highway, but a group of gracious, wonderful people hungry for the message of Christ. Iran is a nation with one of the most courteous, educated populations on earth—a population dominated by young adults under the age of thirty, who have repeatedly elected a young, progressive-minded parliament that is constantly vetoed by the oppressive thumbs of a ruling council of mullahs. Jesus expressed His opinion of such religious tyrants in Matthew 23.

In the midst of this darkness, small sparks of hope are growing into flames as Iranians encounter the love of God.

For thirty years, the Iranian powers have been exporting terror and creating disciples of hatred in the name of Allah in nations as distant as Indonesia. This continues even today. Midway through this campaign of strict Islamization, most Iranians who have not fled their nation have begun to grow weary of the grim, slavish, loveless loyalty to Allah demanded by their Islamic state. Except for staged parades and rallies, most of the air has left the balloon brought in by the Ayatollah Khomeini in 1979.

During my visits to Iran, I have been told that the Guardian Council of mullahs, as well as other high religious-political figures holding absolute power, have their own bank accounts in Dubai, where hundreds of millions of dollars are held, never reaching the Iranian people. Their greed remains secure under the name of Allah. How tragic that thousands of mud-block houses easily collapse in the earthquakes of Iran, killing many of the poor, while the non-taxed religious-political leaders collectively grow far wealthier than the Shah they deposed.

Understandably, many desperate Iranians find comfort in the huge amounts of heroin that cross their borders. In January 2006, news agencies began reporting that Iran has the highest percentage of drug addiction in the world, a sign of the hopelessness of the people.

In the West, cities have rescue missions where the desperate may find help at the sign of a cross. In Iran, the sign of a cross around a neck usually means the bearer is an Orthodox Christian. Iranian Muslims know very little about Jesus Christ, but they do know that Orthodox Christians who live in their country have the cultural and legal right to sell and drink alcohol without persecution, while the Muslims do not. Many Muslims appreciate this form of "Christianity" as it is their back door to privately buy liquor.

Yet in the midst of this darkness, small sparks of hope are growing into flames as Iranians encounter the love of God. In one city I gave an office manager whom I had met a New Testament wrapped in gift paper. She hid it in her drawer and ran across the building to talk excitedly with five other women. A few of them began to wave some sheets of paper at me. I walked over, and one of the women said, "Please, sir, we want to have one, too." I provided them with more New Testaments concealed between the pages of Iranian newspapers. They hid them in their black robes as Iranians cannot openly read God's Word.

The following chapters in *Desperate for God* are a small collection of testimonies representing the largest and fastest growing Muslim movement in the world: Muslims in Iran who are converting to Christianity. Many of these Muslim-Background Believers (MBBs) risk everything to come to Christ. No matter what their status, the Islamic state opposes them.

Iranian army colonel Hamid Pourmand was sentenced to three years in prison on February 17, 2005, when it was learned that he was also a lay pastor. He was arrested during a church conference in a sweep where he and dozens of church leaders were taken to jail. Non-Muslims are not permitted to hold positions as military officers. Pourmand, who converted to Christianity from Islam twenty-five years ago, was convicted of religious deception in the Iranian armed forces.

In November 2005, Ghorban Dordi Tourani, a Muslim convert to Christ and a house-church leader, was assassinated. Despite such oppression and persecution, the Good News of the Savior continues to spread across Iran.

In 2006, Iranian president Mahmoud Ahmadinejad angrily declared that there were 500 to 600 new MBBs in

Iran each month. He is wrong. There are many more. These are just a few of their stories.

The names of the individuals in this book have been changed to protect their identities. In their testimonies, which have been translated into English, we have retained awkward expressions and rough grammar to represent their thoughts more accurately. These believers are also new converts, so some of their theological statements will not be doctrinally perfect in the eyes of some readers. But they have Scripture and fellowship and the desire to follow Jesus.

As you read these pages, may you be encouraged by these faithful believers and be moved to pray for Iran.

SEARCHING *for the* SOURCE *of* POWER

୬୧

Hamed

I remember one morning when our fifth-grade class was led to an exhibition of books for sale in our school library. I bought fifty books about history. I was so excited to continue my search. My teacher loved it so much that he gave me a few additional books as a gift. He helped me carry my books. We both had a stack in our arms walking back to the classroom. This was at the beginning of the revolution in Iran in 1980, so these books were not yet forbidden. I liked reading about ideology and about power. I wanted to know how to succeed and also what position people rose to in their own country with their ideology.

Most of my family were actually Communists of Russian descent. Our roots are in Azerbaijan, but mostly from the Ukraine. I thank God at least my Communist parents did not force me to follow any particular religion, but told me that if I wanted to accept a religion, I would have to study very hard to see which one was true. I was a gifted reader. Even back in the second grade, I read an 800-page book about problems of people and unfortunate children, what they face in life. It was my father's book and was printed by the Communist Party of Iran. I was six years old when I started reading these books about Communist philosophy.

The other children's books were full of cartoons and painting. I still have those books. It makes me happy to know where I started and where I am now. I was searching and looking for the truth. Before the Islamic Revolution, I would find other organizations' magazines. I also read a lot of books about the historical personalities in the world.

When I was ten years old, I was handed a little booklet, not even ten pages long, out on the street. The pages were about to fall apart, but I found a picture of Jesus Christ on one of those pages. I liked to paint pictures in my bedroom, so this picture attracted me right away. I later painted this face of Jesus.

A lot of my friends were Christian, Armenian, Catholic, and Orthodox, but I don't remember who handed me this book. Someone was giving these little books to the people, free, in the streets in Isfahan. Looking at the picture, I became interested in reading the material in that booklet. This became one of my favorite books. When we moved to another house, I watched over it, packing it away carefully. I didn't want to lose it. Once I lost it, and I was so mad, but I found out my sister had it mixed up in her things.

From the moment I read that Jesus booklet, I started to search for this God they're all talking about. First of all, I read the Communist books again. But now all I found was a lot of emptiness in them. I discovered that when Lenin wanted to swear, he said, "To God, I swear." Then I went to the other religions to search, starting with historical beliefs in the books of Iran, Japan, India, Lebanon, China, and Brazil. I read all about the religions so I could compare them. Then I started studying space and stars, hypnotism, spirits, and telepathy.

I discovered the difficulties and problems of other religions. I tried to write those down in a notebook. I wrote notes especially about Islam during the heat of this religious revolution where my countrymen were all involved. I talked to a lot of people. Nobody was able to answer the questions I recorded to ask them. There are so many problems even ayatollahs cannot give an answer.

I couldn't find any Bible, so I was very lost. About this time I was given a clear understanding of some verses of the Bible through a magazine, *The Good News* from England. I was thirteen and filled out a form and sent it back to London. For about two or three years, I could get the magazine before Iran blocked such things. In those magazines I eagerly read pieces of the Bible. I tore them out and collected them. Finally, I found a Bible from a retired old Muslim man who sold some books. He gave me a Bible on loan to read. This Bible was in English, maybe Old English. My English was pretty good then, but I still couldn't understand much. I needed to get answers. I tried to defeat the Bible like I had defeated the Koran and other religions. I argued a lot.

The common people, my friends, couldn't answer my questions but were giving me some excuses. I had to go to those who knew more of such things. I decided to go straight to the mullahs, the Islamic teachers. One of my friends had a new ayatollah or mullah and said, "I'll take you over there so you can talk to him." My friend and I took a taxi to this mullah's home. We knocked at the door and entered. My friend had told him earlier that I was coming. He said, "I have a friend who is one of the ethnic minorities. He wants to come see you."

We sat on the floor on a red carpet and leaned against some pillows and blankets. The mullah had shaved his head. They brought us some tea, no food or sweets. From the beginning the mullah started hating me. I asked him many questions about the Koran, about Allah and Satan and their struggles about who was more powerful. Then I pointed to the Koran chapter 3 (The House of Imran) where the third verse says, "If anybody wants to have salvation[1] and enter Heaven, they have to believe in Torah and also in the Bible and in the New Testament." I turned a few more pages to chapter 4, verse 159[2] and said, "Look, in this chapter it is also written that Jesus is present and involved in judging on the day of judgment." I could see the mullah's face getting red.

I continued with him, "When you look at the Koran's chapters, many are named after the animals, insects, sun, stars, or the moon, because they are copied from idol worship. But there are places in the Koran that talk about the power of God and salvation, where Satan is not able to say anything against God's work. It seems mixed up. But in the Bible, I read, 'Whoever delivers Jesus Christ to the nations, I will give them the kingdom, not in this life but the next life. And I give them all the keys of the kingdom, and I'll make their life blessed.'"

My friend who had brought me here was shifting nervously beside me on the rug. His face was also getting red listening to some of the points I brought up. Suddenly the mullah stood up and said, "I don't want to argue with you. Your ideas are not interesting, so I can't talk to you."

I continued to search for the truth. I always believed the real God should have noble characteristics.

I got up and we left the house quickly. I didn't want to cause my friend any problems, but I continued to search for the truth. I always believed the real God should have noble characteristics. The God I wanted couldn't like bad things for His children. He should know everything and know how that person wants to live in the future. This God in my mind would always care for His children.

I still kept looking for a God I could see. I read the books that said gods were creatures from space, and that they made us the shape we are. I thought if this is really the truth, this took great knowledge. So I respected this creator.

I tried to make some relationship with Satan. I used to have a dog and tried calling the spirits to come to him. He'd start barking and stand on his feet. I was thinking maybe this is it. This was kind of entertaining for my friends, but they were also scared. People from other cities, teachers of these spiritual beliefs, would come to see me. I could hypnotize some people and promised them I would show them the next life. All these people came, most of them Muslims. They're telling my friends, "This is just phenomenal." I invited Satan to my room. I'd written on the door of my room the name of the god of the Holy Eye.

I was a student in the university where some of the people around me were Satan worshipers. I wasn't really worshiping Satan, but I was still searching. I just wanted to know if this hypnotic power was from God or was from Satan. My dog would get nervous and run out of the room. Every morning he would come to my door and scratch at the door for his food, but then I didn't see him for a few days. I knew this couldn't be from God, or it should have given me joy.

One of my university friends was really close to becoming a Christian. I always saw him reading the Bible. He was Armenian, and I was surprised to see he had a Bible in our national language of Farsi, not in Armenian, as these are hard to find. I started asking questions. He got really mad and turned to walk the other way. When I kept asking him about Jesus and God, he was really nervous. He knew I was a Muslim. "If you're a Muslim, you can never understand what the Bible says," he told me. "Go back to your own religion." I would laugh and grin at everything he would say to me.

My professor at the university was talking about the different religions of the world. There were forty to fifty students sitting in the room. I was very combative. I raised my hand and rudely challenged him. "You don't know this religion. Why are you lying about it?" The teacher asked me, "Do you know?" I said, "Yeah." "So come up, and teach it for me," he said. This teacher actually wanted to be friends with me and didn't get angry. He could have been connected to the police and the information office. He invited me to visit his home, but I never went.

About that time I learned about a gathering of Christians in an apartment. As I walked over there, I wondered if I could learn more about this Jesus I had painted years ago. I opened the door and sat down with a group who were sitting on the carpet in a circle. Then behind me my Armenian friend walked in; he was so surprised to see me. There I finally received a Farsi Bible. I thought it was really neat. I knew this is the God I was searching for. But there was still a devil or skepticism in me, because I wanted to find something wrong. I discovered that this Bible was like a concrete wall I couldn't penetrate through criticism. I couldn't damage it or even put a scratch in it. Most of all, it gave me peace. In the weeks that followed, I told myself that's what the Word of God is supposed to do. Other religions left me worrying.

Before I really accepted the Lord, my wife and I started reading the Bible together. Her family were not really religious people, yet they were very defensive. Many evenings we had big arguments around the dining room table. Since they were Muslim, they talked about Islam. I openly told them the Koran is a satanic book. Of all the world's religions, only in the Christian religion is God always holy. My wife told me, "Stop it. Don't argue with them!" But I assured her that I loved her family.

I asked them, "Why was the Islamic holy place, the Kaaba in Mecca, originally full of stone idols? And even now, when you go to Mecca for a pilgrimage, it's between the two mountains of Safa and Marwa. This celebration back when Mohammed lived was to worship two idols, one on top of each mountain. What supreme god must have this worship like this for himself?"

In historical literature, I have read that the sign of the moon placed on top of the mosque is because Islam and the Koran swear to the moon and the stars. The word "Allah" is taken from an idol, the highest of the gods, the moon god. There were idols sold in the idol shops and places or houses called "Allah." When Mohammed came to talk about the god that he was worshiping, he eliminated the dozens of gods but kept Al-Ilah, the highest idol. Later the words were connected together and became "Allah." Allah had three goddess daughters who were worshiped then. They were known as the daughters of Al-Ilah. These goddesses represented by stars were Al-Lat, Al-Uzza, and Manat.

Today, millions of Muslims go around the black stone Kaaba in Mecca. Centuries ago inside this stone Kaaba were the many little stone gods. The moon god, Al-Ilah inside the Kaaba, was declared the highest by Mohammed. Today people are still worshiping an idol name. Uninformed Christian translators placed that name as the name for God in many Bibles as a political compromise for Muslims, so it would be easily accepted by our culture. "Allah" is the only name we use today for God. That's the way it is. But we Christians know who our loving Father is.

After my wife and I had read more in the New Testament about the life of Jesus, we felt peace and serenity. We'd sit and talk to each other. I told her, "This is what I've been looking for all these years. I have searched through so much material all these years. I'm going to accept this." She had been next to me in a spiritual search all these years, but I didn't know it. I took her hand, "Let's go together right now, and together let's believe Jesus."

> OF ALL THE WORLD'S RELIGIONS, ONLY IN THE CHRISTIAN RELIGION IS GOD ALWAYS HOLY.

We didn't know exactly what to say or what to do. I called my wife's uncle in another country, because he was a Christian. We told him we wanted to become Christians. He said, "Wait until I come to Iran." He would be coming in three to four months. This was a good time for my wife and I because we kept reading the Bible. We talked together and built each other up through the words in its pages. We didn't know any Christians very well in our city—only the few Armenians I met in the apartment—and we didn't know about any churches where non-Armenian Muslim-background believers like us could sit and not draw any attention.

We continued to pray as best we knew how. Finally, one morning the phone rang. My wife's uncle was in Iran. We rode on a bus 700 kilometers (435 miles) to meet him. When we arrived, he met us at the station and told us, "I have another guest who will be coming. He will talk to you. Then he can give you baptism." We pulled our bags off the bus and went to stay with the uncle at his friend's house. We had much, much joy and interest. I always carried my Bible with me, but for security we didn't bring our own Bibles on this journey.

For a few days, we visited different places in their beautiful city. We talked to the uncle about Jesus Christ and how we found Him. He saw we really knew about the Bible, but then he had a final examination for me. One night at dinner he turned and asked, "Who is Jesus to you? What do you think about Jesus Christ? Who is He?" This took me by surprise. What kind of question is this?

I stopped eating. I didn't understand his question. I had read so many books, but this was very personal. I asked, "Would you open up this question a little more so I can know what you're talking about?" Uncle said, "How do you know Him? What happened that you know Him? Is He the Son of God?" I replied, "Jesus is God, Savior, and for years He's the person I've been searching for. What I have built and searched for in my mind about God, it just matches." He asked a few more questions. My wife, sitting beside me, nodded her head in agreement.

We pushed our chairs back and gathered together. A Christian in the group prayed for my wife and me. I don't remember what the prayer was. But this was the first time another Christian had prayed for us. It was a special time. Then the uncle said, "You're ready to get baptized."

We brought a change of clothes for after we got wet. We got baptized in the tub at someone's house. They began filling the tub with water. There wasn't a lot of room, so the group knelt beside the tub. Others stood in the doorway. My wife and I prayed as we each got in the water. After the baptism, they said a prayer.

While drying my hair, I began shaking, and I started crying with joy. I knew I was ready to serve God at that time. I wasn't really worrying about someone hearing the news of my baptism. We started sharing right away. I really wanted to tell everybody, my family and my wife's family.

My wife was really scared of my brother and family. She said, "Don't say anything about it in our family." I told her, "I don't care. It's so important to me that we found the real God. And I'm certain it won't take long until everybody knows we're Christians."

I have received a lot of miracles from Jesus in my life. After our baptism, I called my mom who lives on the other side of Iran. My side of the family didn't know anything about the Bible. I held the phone, ready to give her the news, but first my mother said, "I dreamed something strange." I asked, "What did you dream?" Mom asked me,

"Are you becoming a Christian?" I was really shocked. She didn't even know we were reading the Bible. She said, "I dreamed last night you were sitting on a big high chair with a robe and a lot of spiritual people were around you. Most of them were praying, and a lot of them were singing some songs. Then I saw another man there. He had a religious robe on, and I asked him, 'What's going on in here? Why is my son sitting on that high chair?' And the man said, 'Your son became a Christian, and this celebration is for him.'"

I was really surprised when Mom said that. This was a confirmation from her. That made me happier and even more stable in my belief, in my faith. A few days later, my wife and I tearfully left this loving group where we were baptized. We hid a stack of Bibles in our bags and climbed on the bus for the long ride back home.

I changed the way I talked to my wife's family after I became a Christian. I didn't try to make them angry or defensive with intellectual arguments, but I began emphasizing that I'm a Christian. My wife said, "Don't tell them now; it's too soon." While serving tea, her eyes got big when I was confessing to them. Her brother is a very fanatical Muslim, so I was very careful. I would ask her brother, "Are you mad at me ... in a bad way or in a loving way?" I didn't want to force my belief on him. They still got mad, but I was not. I was smiling.

He was really blind in his fanaticism. He told me, "Whatever you tell me, even if it's truth, and you tell me Islam will take me down to the pit and I'll just really fall into the deep well, still I will stand on my word." Then he put his cup down and declared, "You're going to destroy yourself."

I replied, "Okay, but because I love you, I'm telling you this truth about Jesus. Listen, I just want you to go study. Don't read only the books that are for Islam, but also read the books against Islam. Read philosophy and then read the Bible and see what it says." I was not afraid for him to follow the same path I had, as long as he finally encountered the Bible. Even after his hard words, he accepted this approach and is beginning to read. He has a big library and is starting his own search.

> WHEREVER I GO, I START TALKING ABOUT JESUS... WHATEVER WE TALK ABOUT, I TURN THESE SUBJECTS TO GOD.

After three months back home, we found a few Christians in our city. They had learned about us, and one day they came to our house. We were so happy to meet them, a new part of our family. But I hadn't been sitting still before this time. Wherever I go, I start talking about Jesus. If I am sitting in the bus and see a person next to me, I can't just sit still. I begin talking. Whatever we talk about—nature, mountains, science, or things like that—I turn these subjects to God. God has given me this talent, a gift. From everything, even a small word, I build a big rope for them to reach God.

Now when I talk to people, they never get mad. Sometimes I bring humor into it. Sometimes they gratefully talk to me about their secrets. In a short time, they come back to me and talk about their difficulties, sicknesses, and sorrows. I take those difficulties and begin to show them Jesus Christ. In my briefcase I always have five or six New Testaments and a Bible.

My wife also shares the gospel with people. One Muslim uncle of hers said, "You're going to get yourself killed one of these days." I think God is going to protect our family, our children, as He has always protected the believers. God is still in that business.

Before we were Christians, we didn't want children but just wanted a good time. Yet today we are blessed by a little daughter and son. My favorite Bible verse is, "Come all you who labor and have a heavy load, and I'll give you rest" (Matthew 11:28). The next ones I like are about the Kingdom in John chapter 8 where Jesus came to set us free.

Today society won't let you into places that you want to go if you don't have enough knowledge. Or if you want to go to a kingdom or a palace, you still have to have an important contact before they let you in. But in Jesus' Kingdom, you have the power to walk in with no higher knowledge or contacts. You can come in very comfortably and don't have to act religious or work your way in to reach your King. The King has already given you the right and the directions to serve Him. Now I think this was God's plan from the beginning of my life to really search, to see and read all this religion. This has helped me with others.

I work from 5:30 a.m. to 8:00 p.m. in a large factory where there is an assembly line. We have been Christians for four years now. Our town is so fanatical we can only worship as a family in our apartment right now. But the other day, I witnessed to a shop owner on my side of the family. I have gone to his shop in the evening after it is closed, and we turn off the light and sing and pray there. Our family is faithful. God will carry us through.

Notes:

1 The word "salvation" comes from the word *furqān* in Arabic. This is also translated as "criterion" in some versions of the Koran.

2 Verse numbers vary in different translations of the Koran.

PADINA *in the* HOUSE *of* ZEINAB

☙❧

Padina

I stared at the cluster of sleeping pills in my hand. What else could I do? A failed marriage, rejected by our closed society after my divorce, the terrible shame I had brought on my family, my mother dying of multiple sclerosis. I couldn't go on any longer. Killing myself seemed like the only escape from my pain. I tossed the pills into my mouth, washed them down with a glass of water, and waited for the peace I so desperately craved.

At an early age, I'd committed myself to the only god I knew—Allah. If I could do all the things he demanded, he would answer my prayers, give me peace, and someday allow me to enter his paradise. When I turned fourteen, I joined a *Zeinabiyeh* (the House of Zeinab), where women can study the Koran and learn how to better please Allah. While this House was dedicated to Imam Hazrat Zeinab, we prayed to many imams.

My parents, especially my father, and relatives didn't want me to join. For a time I hid my activities from them. Before long my dedication drew attention, and I rose in the *Zeinabiyeh* to the position of serving in the sacred place where twelve imams, the holy men of Islam, were worshiped. I moved up to the level where I served and worshiped Hazrat Zeinab, the sister of Imam Hussein, and then I advanced to the top level. With the help of my teachers, this level allowed me to study, memorize, and translate small parts of the Koran from Arabic—the language of Mohammed—into Farsi, which is what most Iranians speak.

During the seven years I attended the *Zeinabiyeh*, I awoke every morning at one o'clock to pray. I would climb out of the top bunk of my bed, while my younger sister slept on the bottom bunk. Rather than sit at our small desk or on the sofa in our room, I would place a cloth on the floor in the center of the room, light my candle, sit down and pray until 5:00 a.m.

At dawn, during good weather, I would climb up to the roof and continue my prayers. Seven days a week I would pray for each of the imams and their families, one at a time.

After I completed my morning prayers, I would attend school all day long and then go to the Zeinab House followed by more prayers. At five o'clock, we would pray the prayers all Muslims pray five times a day. If we had no work to do, we continued to pray. Sometimes after a special program, I would be there until midnight, go home and sleep for an hour or two before beginning the next day's prayer session.

Following the teaching time and prayers, we would go into a time of grieving for the dead prophets. For this we wore black. Because of my zeal, my teachers gave me an armband noting I'd been especially chosen for this activity.

On Tuesday I would meet with 400 other women, starting at 2:00 p.m., and pray until 9:00 p.m. Our ages ranged from five years old to ninety. Parents would bring their young girls, as it was important for them to know the Koran and to learn how to honor Allah.

We would loudly sing special songs grieving for dead imams. When everyone left, I would get a hand broom and rags to clean the house and do the dishes as my greater service to Allah. Having to bend over so long to sweep the floors has produced back, neck, and shoulder problems to this day.

On days we didn't have general meetings, we met in smaller groups throughout the house. Persian rugs covered the floor, their patterns muted by years of prayer. Large cushions lined the walls to rest our backs on. For special prayers, we entered a smaller room where we opened a sliding wooden door, and then stepped beyond a thick green curtain and a thin green net into a closet-sized room. Once inside, we would knot the green cloth around a notch in the door to symbolize making a covenant with the imams for answered prayer. Pictures of the imams lined the walls. If we held a special service in honor of one of the imams, for their birthday or to mourn for them, we would leave the sliding door and the curtains open so that we could see their pictures on the walls inside the little room.

As part of my service to Allah, I cleaned the rooms after everyone left. In the small room dedicated to the imams, I washed the glass picture frames with rosewater. While I cleaned the pictures, I'd make my own prayers and requests of the imams, always expecting an answer to my prayers.

Women would fall down and tear at their faces. Others would bang their heads on the floor and pull out their hair.

On one of the special days, we filled a large metal tub with water and closed it for fifteen days. During that time, we bowed in front of the tub and read Koranic verses, grieving for the imams. After fifteen days, we opened the lid and poured the water into little glass bottles, which we handed to the people. The worshipers would cry and mourn.

Some very dark celebrations included large parades in the streets. The mourners, all men, marched in long lines and beat themselves with chains. Women couldn't walk in these parades or even watch. We couldn't even see the men go out the door. We performed the same rituals as the men behind the walls of our homes. We women formed circles and began grieving. In the middle of the circles, women would fall down and tear at their faces. Others would bang their heads on the floor and pull out their hair. On one particular holiday, we would beat our chests so hard that we'd be painfully black and blue. Following the grieving ritual, we would cook food and give it to the poor people and then we'd offer prayers asking Allah to do something for them, whatever they asked.

We believed that when we prayed for the dead imams, we prayed to Allah. As a young girl, my mind would often wander when I prayed. My spiritual zeal lessened, and although I became sick of the routine, I feared I would be punished if I stopped. Many of the girls got sick and became depressed.

Imam Khomeini, our guiding saint, issued instructions for all the Zeinab Houses that we shouldn't listen to music. We could only watch a little closed-circuit television. There we could see people circling the Kaaba, the black stone of Mecca, as they sang their grieving funeral songs. The imam said he was doubtful we should even hear those songs. He refused to allow us to attend weddings or parties, and to socialize in mixed company.

To keep us pure, we couldn't see any foreign movies. When asked why, they said, "Because men wear sleeveless clothing and women wear short skirts. Your eyes will be messed up."

Our teachers taught us that Imam Zaman, who had mysteriously disappeared, would reappear at the end of time and Jesus would be right behind him. Together they would establish a new kingdom. This gave me a glimmer of hope for the future.

Historically, many of the imams had been attacked and imprisoned. To grieve for them, we would join with 150 others, put cloths on our heads with the name of a specific imam on it, and put ropes around our waists, linking us together. Then we'd march around the outside of our house, putting mud on our heads, crying and hitting ourselves. We thought this would earn Allah's favor.

My sins were ever before me. I would remember days when I'd been terrible. I knew Allah must be angry at me. I feared dying and being judged so much that I refused to think about it. Even Mohammed's daughter so feared Allah that, when he'd visit her, she would cry a container full of tears. If one so pure feared dying, how could I expect to get into heaven? I knew there was no way I could cry a whole container full of tears.

I had nightmares about dying. I'd been taught that when a dead person went underground all the dead spirits attacked him if he didn't believe in the twelve imams and pray to them, or if he wasn't good enough. So, every day when I'd worship and cry, I'd bring a handkerchief to collect my tears. When Imam Zaman returned, I would be able to show him, "Look, I shed all these tears for you."

For seven years the *Zeinabiyeh* dominated my life. Yet nothing changed. I tried so hard. I searched for peace within my religion but found none. Instead everything worsened, including my depression. I feared that if any of my hair stuck out of my scarf, Allah would hang me from my hair in heaven forever. We wore stockings on our hands to prevent our hands from being exposed, even a little bit. They told us that we would be hung by our hands in heaven. Heavy black socks covered my legs. If I accidentally revealed my ankles to anyone, Allah would drop me repeatedly in hell to burn my legs. I could reach heaven only if I wore all this stuff and cried all the time. Finally, a young woman of twenty-one, I left the Zeinab House. My studies were complete. They had shown me a very bad god, an angry god.

Earlier, when I turned eighteen, a young man had asked for my hand in marriage and my father agreed. Navid had been educated in Europe and Iran. When he informed my father that he wished to study overseas, my father said, "You go ahead. We'll keep Padina for you until you return and can have a real engagement and wedding."

If I accidentally revealed my ankles to anyone, Allah would drop me repeatedly in hell to burn my legs.

When I met him at the ceremony where he officially asked for my hand in marriage, I fell in love with him. Somebody chose me, somebody loves me! Navid arranged for me to stay at his parents' house during his absence so no one could touch me while he was gone. This meant that I was limited in how often I could visit my home or the homes of my loved ones.

I prayed to Allah for Navid's safety. As a good Muslim, I couldn't go directly to Allah. I needed to go to Imam Hussein and bribe him with good deeds and gifts, trying to get Imam to make Navid call me. When Navid didn't call, I thought I must have done something wrong.

Navid continued to claim to be getting his masters degree. Once he returned for a year. Since we lived together for two months without being married, my relatives branded me as an immoral woman. However, because our marriage had never been formally completed, he did not need to officially divorce me when he left again.

Receiving no financial support from Navid, I found a job as a medical assistant where I worked from seven in the morning to seven at night. At the end of my workday, I would do my prayer beads, say my five prayers and fall into bed, only to do it all over again the next day.

The work helped me not to think about my pain and my situation. But my depression deepened. The medical staff with whom I worked noticed. When I complained about not being able to sleep at night, the doctors prescribed sleeping pills. When the pills failed to work, they prescribed even stronger drugs.

I became friends with a Christian Armenian nurse at the hospital. Her stability and peace impressed me. When someone died others would cry, but not her. She'd ask, "Why do you cry? They've gone to a better place." Another thing I noticed about my Christian friend was that when the nurses gossiped about the other workers, she would not participate. Even when pressured, she refused to participate.

When I asked for time off work to attend one of the Muslim grieving holidays, she insisted that I come to work. From a window I watched and mentally joined in when a parade of worshipers plastered their heads with mud and beat their bodies as they marched past the hospital. I returned to the nurses' station and my friend asked, "So did you grieve for this imam and that imam today?"

"Of course," I replied.

"I don't know how you can be a Muslim. If I tell you something you won't be upset, will you?"

"No." I treasured her friendship.

"How is it that you folks can stand around the nurses' station and judge other people? You break people's hearts and then pray for Imam Hussein."

Not having an answer, I asked, "What do you people [Christians] do?"

"We have one God. He has one Son—Jesus Christ. We have only one special day a year. We just wear our regular clothes and we don't grieve. You guys constantly grieve for a thousand different imams."

Her answer intrigued me; I grew curious to learn more.

After I'd worked at the hospital for three years, Navid returned. He apologized to my parents for putting me through so much. "I want to marry her and restore her reputation." To me, he said, "Everywhere I go I try to find a relationship with a woman, but I'm never happy. I'm probably destined to be with you."

Two hours later, we signed the legal documents that made us husband and wife. Since I believed that my depression stemmed from my failed marriage and ruined reputation, I thought it would disappear now that I'd realized my five-year-old dream. It worked for a time, until Navid decided to return to Canada. I discovered he'd wed a Canadian woman in order to get his citizenship papers.

He said they'd never consummated the marriage. The woman refused to divorce him; she wanted revenge. When I asked why he couldn't apply for me to join him, he would tell me that if Canada found out he had another wife, they wouldn't grant his citizenship.

"Don't worry," he'd say, "I'm coming back for you one of these days. I'm working hard to build a big life for us."

My husband's family blamed me that Navid wouldn't come back home to stay. They said, "You must be doing something wrong."

I did everything I could to make them like me. Finally Navid said, because I'd been so kind to them, he was coming back for a month. His month back in Iran brought up a lot of problems and issues between us. I tried to compromise so he would stay in my life. He insisted that I give up my job and forsake all contact with my friends. He discouraged me from even attending family weddings. Because I was living with his family, my activities became more and more limited. His control over me intensified. My depression and inability to sleep worsened.

One evening, I watched a televised church service where the pastors sang, "Jesus is my light, Jesus is my light."

The camera swung around the room showing different people. Everyone looked so happy. Little children jumped up and down, singing and clapping their hands. Even the old people raised their hands in joy. *Can this be?* I wondered. *Aren't they supposed to cry?*

A baptismal service followed. I'd never seen anything like it. I learned baptism meant that all of your sins had been washed away, that you died with Jesus, were raised to a new life, and were completely forgiven. My mind constantly told me how awful I was and how sinful I'd been. Yet, this program said I could be free of all that.

I wanted to be happy like those people. Trapped in the house, I began regularly watching the program. I compared the preachers to Imam Khomeini who never cracked a smile. Islamic holy men on Iranian TV sit hour after hour looking very sad and criticizing other countries. The people on this new TV show appeared happy, peaceful, even joyous. *What is the difference?* I wondered. When an international number appeared on the screen, I made a call. I asked to speak to the man with the white hair, Pastor Hormouz. They took my call over the air. I asked them why they were so happy. They shared with me about Jesus.

The next week an Iranian lady gave me a Bible. I was so surprised. I hesitated opening it for fear the god of my religion would send me to hell. In the next year my life began to change. On the phone, my relationship with Navid improved.

Each time I would lay out my prayer rug, I would face toward Mecca and pray as I'd always done. When I finished, I would pray to Jesus. I reasoned that I didn't pray to Him as God, but as a prophet or a person on a higher level, a mediator. To me, He was another imam.

For one whole year, every time I prayed to Jesus, He would work on my behalf. Previously, I'd fasted and prayed and never received a blessing, only curses. When I began to pray to Jesus, I would go to my window and say, "Jesus, I really need You. I need this from You." And it would happen without my doing anything to make it happen.

Every night at 10:00, I would sit before the TV to learn more about Christianity. But, whenever the preachers said Jesus was God, I'd change the channel. I'd been taught that Christians were infidels. They didn't respect God. If they touched any food, good Muslims shouldn't eat it. They were dirty, unclean fanatics.

Once I began reading the Bible, I couldn't get enough of it. I went to my Armenian friend, even though I'd been forbidden to do so by Navid. She would answer my questions. Other times I would call the program.

I couldn't understand how these people could love a God who is supposed to be angry and scary. I became obsessed with the program, with the love I saw in their faces. There they were, old and enjoying life, yet I was young and not enjoying my life. I'd built religious walls around myself, causing my heart to become very hard. But one day I called the program. This time they recognized my voice.

The pastor asked, "Padina, so who is Christ to you?"

Stunned that they called me by my first name (in Islamic society I would be addressed by my family name), I stammered through my tears, "I see Jesus as someone who is light, the Light of God who has been divided off from God."

We talked a while, and then he prayed for me. I felt so blessed. From that moment I knew Jesus was far more than an imam or a prophet. Once a week I called and prayed for peace. As I watched the nightly programs, my fear of God lessened. When the month of Ramadan arrived, I called the pastor. I didn't know what to do. Should I follow the fasting and rituals, or not? After talking it over with him, I decided I wouldn't.

Will Allah hit me? Is he angry with me? Will he kill me? Will he hurt my family?

My mother, a very religious woman and committed to Islam, had MS for several years. The doctors said she'd be paralyzed soon, her lungs would swell, and she would die. When I told her about the TV program, she watched it with me. The first time she saw it she exclaimed, "That's it! That's what I've been looking for."

My mother's illness and my mess of a marriage intensified my depression. In the middle of this, my husband returned for a month. He had no sense of the fact that my mother was dying. He acted unconcerned. For the last four years I'd been his wife, but he'd never received me as his wife. Continually he promised, "I'm busy right now, but I'm coming back and will take you with me to Canada pretty soon."

> *F*ROM THAT MOMENT I KNEW JESUS WAS FAR MORE THAN AN IMAM OR A PROPHET.

We disagreed over everything. I couldn't get him to understand how upset I was over my mother. It didn't bother him for me to know he was always trying to pick up girls. When he went back to Canada he called immediately, "I can see that we have no connection so let's let this thing go. Let's get a divorce."

When he added that he didn't want me anymore, I couldn't speak. I'd invested ten years of my life in him. Nothing could have been worse for my mother to hear. Stress makes MS worse. My parents learned about the divorce and they became upset. They had always backed him. They couldn't believe that he wanted a divorce. My mother's health worsened, as did my depression. That's the night I decided to end it all.

I had barely swallowed the pills when my mother got up off her bed. The instant she saw me she knew I'd done something bad.

"Did you take pills?"

I lied.

"Yes, you did!" She immediately made me drink yogurt, which made me throw up.

My response to her saving my life was, "Mom, you can make me stop this time and I'll throw up, but I'll try again."

With my mind made up to take my life one way or another, I stopped watching the Christian TV program. One night when my sister turned on the television, she turned up the volume so high that it resonated throughout the house. I immediately recognized the theme song. My mother got out of bed to watch it.

The topic was about people who took medication for depression and how to escape it. While my sister wondered why anyone would do such a thing, my mother and I wept for joy to finally find an answer to my depression. At the end of the program my mother called in to pray with the preacher. Then she handed the phone to me.

I didn't want to take the phone. In my mind, I believed no one cared. Can he bring Navid back to me? Can he give my mother good health? Finally, I reached for the phone. With the coldest heart and voice I started talking to him.

The kindness in his voice broke something inside of me. I started crying. I told him everything.

"Your mom told me that you tried to commit suicide. Why would you do that? Don't you value yourself? Don't you know how much God loves you? Don't you know that Jesus wants to save you from all that?"

"No! What can He do for me? He can't do anything for me."

He asked me several questions and I gave him a lot of answers. Finally he said, "So, you've tried everything your religion has to offer, right?"

"Yeah, and none of it has given me an answer back. How does Jesus want to save me, how can He save me? No one can keep me from trying again to kill myself."

"Okay, so you're going to kill yourself. There's nothing I can do about it, but will you do one thing for me first? Will you try one more thing?" He didn't give me time to reply. "Put off killing yourself for a few more days so you can get to know the God I know and see what you think. I'll show you how you can know Jesus personally. You can walk with Him for a few days. See how He treats you and how He is. If Jesus doesn't do anything for you, for your depression, then you can go kill yourself."

"Pastor, my life is so messed up, how can God possibly undo all the bad stuff?"

"Put it to the test and you'll see." As he prayed for me, I could hear in his voice that he was crying and that he really cared for me. By the end of the prayer I was sobbing too. I cried and prayed and repented of my sins.

A few weeks later, a Christian woman called and invited my mother and me to her home. We began meeting together and studying Christianity. Afraid I'd stray into some crazy religion again, I had many questions. Whenever I had questions, I would call the television program for answers. They answered each of my questions until I felt safe.

After the pastor's prayer and after my questions had been answered, I had a faith in Christ that could not be moved. I finally knew Jesus Christ had saved me. I could risk being happy. My mother came to the same decision for herself. We started attending church and our peace began to flow. So did the miracles.

My mother stopped taking the cortisone shots for her MS and got out of bed. She'd been healed. Her doctors were amazed and asked, "Where did the MS go?" Seeing my mother healed brought my father to Jesus. My sister came to know Jesus, too. We watched the TV programs as a family.

I stopped taking the pills for sleeping and depression. None! I have the best sleep at night. I am happy all the time. Nothing bothers me. I am filled with joy. My Armenian nurse friend rejoiced with me. "Don't worry, I'll be with you all the way, whatever happens."

All the love and devotion I tried to give to my husband, the love he could never return, I give now to Jesus. In return, He gives me patience. It's amazing! Since our family got saved and we've been set free, everything in our lives is back to a place where it is supposed to be. We have new friends who love us and we love them. Everyone saw my mom's healing and they say I am so different too. Because of my family's testimony, many family and friends are coming to Christ.

Every Thursday night we invite people into our home for dinner. After dinner, while we sit around talking and sipping tea, we turn on the television and we say, "Oh, what a nice program. I wonder what it is?" And everybody starts watching it with us. They get glued to the television. Eighty percent of the people that we've introduced to Jesus have found Jesus through this television program. Tears roll down their faces and we encourage them to call in. At the end of their calls, they say, "By the way, Padina says hello."

These people know I attended the Islamic schools for so long that I memorized the Koran and became involved in the higher levels of the school. When I point out places in the Koran where it contradicts itself, they trust me because they know I know what I'm talking about. I gave my life for it.

One month ago my divorce from Navid became final. I didn't tell him I'd become a Christian. I struggled to forgive him. When I'd discussed my anger with the pastor, he'd say, "If you don't forgive him, you will not have the closeness with God that you want."

I tried, but the hatred returned to my heart. Sometimes I would send him hateful e-mails. One night on the program they said, "Forgiveness works like this. Even if you're the victim, you have to go and find the person and tell them that you forgive them for anything they've done against you."

For the next week I was in a spiritual battle. I couldn't stop thinking about forgiving Navid. God had touched my heart. I called the program and told them I just couldn't forgive him and that's just the way it was.

They answered, "If you don't forgive him, think of how unlike Christ you are being. He hung on the cross and was tortured by these people. But He kept His peace. He said nothing."

"But you don't understand. I waited for Navid for so many years."

"Christ did that and more for you. On the cross Jesus said to forgive them, for they didn't know what they were doing. Isn't this the same thing? You haven't suffered more than Jesus, have you? You can't show me any reason why you shouldn't forgive."

Together we prayed a prayer of forgiveness. It touched my heart so deeply that I got on the Internet and wrote to Navid, "I ask your forgiveness for all the ugly and hateful things I said and felt."

Shortly after I finally forgave Navid, they had a seminar in the house church about knowing God. Before, whenever they studied the concept of knowing God face to face I would pass out. Worried for me, a group picked me up and carried me into another room and started praying for me. My arms hung limp. I couldn't move them. Weak and exhausted, I asked them to let me rest in the darkened room. I felt terrible. Suddenly I heard a voice say, "Get up!"

At first I thought I was hearing things, but the voice spoke again. "Get up!"

I didn't move, so it called to me again, clearer and louder this time. Without opening my eyes my body raised up off the bed, not in the usual manner of sitting up and then pushing yourself to your feet. It was like someone picked up my shoulders and I just stood straight up. My pastor, my church leader, and another person who had helped bring me into the room got scared.

I sat down on the edge of the bed in disbelief. "What happened?"

Again the voice spoke. "Get up!"

As I stood to my feet in obedience, my head hung limp on my chest. Then I saw Jesus. He stood in the room with me. I saw His robes and His feet. Suddenly, I knew I'd been delivered from my hatred. He did it Himself. The unrest from my problems, my depression, my failed marriage, melted away. Joy filled my life. Before long I'd almost forgotten there had ever been a Navid.

> THEN I SAW JESUS. HE STOOD IN THE ROOM WITH ME. SUDDENLY, I KNEW I'D BEEN DELIVERED FROM MY HATRED.

Iranians have a sweetness toward Christ. One Sunday we got into a taxi to go to an Armenian church. I noticed that the driver had rings on his fingers, each with the name of a different imam on it. I had no doubt but that the man took the grieving holidays quite seriously. We talked about Jesus with him during the ride. As he dropped us off, he asked, "Go and tell Jesus about me and pray for me over there."

Islam is a religion of depression and pills. It turns people into walking zombies. I would so love to speak to the girls attending the higher levels of the Islamic schools. I could sit right there and show them that I have what they want. I know the scriptures of the Koran. I've done all the things they do. I've prayed all the prayers they pray. I did it all, but found no peace from Allah or from Islam. I would tell them to test Jesus, to see what He will do in their lives. I would love to tell all the people of Iran about the beautiful Jesus I have seen. I know how tired and depressed they are and they have the same problems as I had. I know how hopeless they feel.

I WOULD LOVE TO TELL ALL THE PEOPLE OF IRAN ABOUT THE BEAUTIFUL JESUS I HAVE SEEN . . . I KNOW HOW HOPELESS THEY FEEL.

I want to give my whole life to Christ. I want to surrender everything to Him. I no longer worry about who will do what to me. God has replaced my nightmares with a vision for myself and for other people.

WHO IS JESUS?

❦

Yasmin

During the Islamic revolution in 1979, there was a curfew. No one was supposed to be on the street at night. My mom, pregnant with me, was in labor and she had to walk alone in the dark, step by step to the doctor. Pausing at the street corner, she didn't know the way. The police saw her and thought there was something wrong, so they took her to the police station.

My father, who was a drug addict, had stayed at home, unable to go with her. The police went back to our house to pick him up and drove them both to the hospital.

Mom saw the sign on the hospital: "Son of Mary Hospital." She started praying to Jesus, so she would have an easy delivery. She knew little about Jesus, but she needed help. She also prayed for her husband to be free from drugs.

The police car stopped at the main entrance. When they opened the car door, my father just fell out onto the sidewalk and couldn't get up. Mother walked slowly up the hospital steps still praying to this Jesus. Father lay unconscious outside until morning.

Later, when Mother woke up in bed, she looked up at the nurse beside her. "Where's my baby? Why don't you start delivering my baby?" she asked. The nurse pointed, "Look! The baby is already delivered and is sleeping right next to you. Now don't turn over on the baby because you might suffocate her." I am happy that my mother said I came into this world giving no pain or ache to her. I weighed three kilos (6.6 pounds).

At thirteen years old, I wondered if God existed in other religions. I didn't want the Allah of Islam.

My father was in jail for two years. I had a hard time and a hard life without him. When I was nine years old, because of the Islamic revolution, they forced me not to paint my fingernails or wear any makeup. I thought, *Why are they doing this to me? What does this have to do with God—not painting my nails, or having to cover my hair and wear the big black robe? What kind of help is this to me? What kind of a relationship is this to God?* I had a lot of difficulties. My mother had some depression, my father was still sick.

I wanted to get closer to God. One day I thought if I cover my hair, every strand, I can get closer. But I wasn't fulfilled at all. I fasted some days trying to get closer to God, but that didn't help. I didn't know anything about Jesus. I thought in my heart, *I don't have anyplace in this world.* I was lost. I didn't like Islam, and I didn't know what was going to happen. At thirteen years old, I wondered if God existed in other religions. I didn't want the Allah of Islam.

I could not find a way, so I became full of hate. It was difficult because my father was again in jail. I was reading the Muslim prayers, but all those rituals didn't do anything for me, nor did reading religious books and the Koran, and all those verses. I used to close the Koran and go to my bedroom and cry. There was no God for me.

I always felt guilty because I wasn't following the Koran's commandments, but at least I tried to find some peace. My bedroom was not a nice-looking room. We were living with my grandpa in his very old home. Grandpa had a lot of wives. He gave a room to each one of his wives, so our family slept in one room. Now home from jail, my father kept using heroin. It was so painful for me to see him take our money to buy heroin and then sit in the corner of our room and inject it. Sometimes he asked me to tie the rope on his arm.

One corner of the room was full of our dishes in stacks on the floor because we didn't have a kitchen. I didn't grumble. I was a really quiet girl when I was at that age. We had a little closet, a wardrobe in the corner. To get away from my folks, I climbed into that closet to hide. I always shut the door when my father began putting the needle in his arm. In the dark closet, I put my head down on my knees. I began talking to what I hoped was God. I asked, "God, why am I having such a life? My father should be working. My mother should have a kitchen, a nice life, a home." All of us, my brother and sisters too, were sleeping in one room—six people on the floor.

My mother and father were not religious. They didn't read the Koran or believe in anything. Although I didn't have a prayer rug, I still prayed in the Islamic way five times a day. When we cooked, the smoke from the little kerosene burner made tears come in my eyes while I prayed. My throat was sore all the time. Later, when my grandfather died, we received some money, and we bought a home on payments. Now, all the women sleep in one room and the men in another.

A year ago we put a coat over my father's funny little pajamas to take him to a doctor so he could get some medicine and quit using heroin. We didn't have money to go to a big hospital doctor. Getting him to a clinic was tough. My dad didn't want to go to the clinic that morning. He wanted some money to go buy more heroin. So I hid my money in my clothes so he wouldn't see it. My father thought we were going to take him to the crazy house, the sanitarium. He didn't want to go with us, but we got him into a taxi. Around noon, the doctors came into this inexpensive clinic. I sat on a bench crying.

While sitting on the bench, I reviewed my circumstances. I was nineteen years old and ready to go to the university, but my life was falling in on me. My brother was really abusing me and abusing my mom and my dad. He was a really rebellious brother. The police came in our house from time to time because of the heroin. They were just really bothering me and badmouthing me. They were angry that we even took Father to their jail again looking for help. They told us to stop this. All our remedies for him to quit heroin had not worked out.

Finally, it was my turn to see the secretary of the doctor, sitting in her office. We found out he's a very good doctor, very reasonable, and everybody recommended him.

At first I didn't like him and was disappointed. I thought the clinic would be a very big organization, but I just saw one table and three white chairs. I thought, *What kind of a clinic is this?*

Dr. Alam looked kindly at us, asked questions and took some notes, then gave us a bottle and said, "Here are some of these pills." My dad mumbled and shook his head. He didn't want to take the pills. He wanted some special pills that had more drugs in them. I learned that this doctor was a Christian. I was studying other religions, but I was so afraid to ask about Jesus. (There's a bookstore near his clinic that has some Zoroastrian books. I read about Zoroastrianism and bought more books about other religions, but still was so afraid to ask right then about Jesus.) So the doctor said, "Take him home. I'll come visit him at your house."

Our house wasn't really looking too good right then, so I took him to my grandma's home. Dr. Alam came and started giving him a calcium shot, but all his veins were plugged up and the liquid couldn't go through. He put the syringe down. We didn't know what else to do. We told the doctor, "We don't have much money." He said, "Don't worry about it. God's going to help you. I'm not going to charge you." We told him we're going to pay him by payments. He replied, "No, there's a God who's going to watch out for you." When he said that, I kind of changed my mind about him. I thought, *He's a good man, a really humble person.*

I found out that Dr. Alam was very lenient on the fees, so each morning after my prayers, I took a bus and walked in to sit on the bench. I discussed different problems that my father and I had. One morning when I walked in, the doctor's wife was sitting there. She brought her children to the clinic every day after school. She looked at me and said, "God wants your father to be healed." I thought she was saying that only to make me happy. I was so surprised that she would talk to me. She was so humble and not too remote from people like us.

"Why, even on the cross, do our Muslim leaders say Jesus is coming back with our prophet, Mohammed?"

Soon after this, I started university. I wanted to be Dr. Alam's secretary. We became really good friends. I went to their home one day and saw that they had no pictures of the prophets on their walls. I stopped looking around and asked her why. She said, "Those pictures don't bring me any happiness. They don't really do me any good or meet my needs." She opened a drawer and took out a video. It was about the life of Jesus.

I went over to my grandma's house and put the movie into her VCR. Then I sat on the carpet and watched the movie. I saw them make fun of Jesus and try to trap Him. I thought, *Well, Jesus was just like me. He had a lot of hard times.*

I kept watching the movie to know what would happen at the end. I wanted to do the wonderful things that Jesus did. But they killed Him. I started crying at the end of the movie. I said, "Why, after all that He did, did they put Him on the cross?"

I started asking questions about Jesus and that movie. I couldn't understand the whole thing really. After He went on the cross, it was finished. I had so many questions in my mind. First, I asked some Muslims. They told me, "Well, He's going to come back with our prophet Mohammed, together." Then I went to the doctor's wife and asked her, "Why, even on the cross, do our Muslim leaders say Jesus is coming back with our prophet, Mohammed?" This was the moment that she gave me a Bible.

I gathered the rest of our family to watch the video. We were all sitting there on the floor watching it. My brother wasn't there, but my sisters were. My sisters had a kind of pity for Jesus. They sighed and made expressions of sympathy. They were so taken by Him and sorry, the whipping and lies told when He was on the cross. My mother watched and said, "I wish I could give Him some water to drink." Then she began crying.

They were amazed, like me, when they saw Jesus appear again to His disciples. When He resurrected and came out of the grave I thought, *He's coming to our home.* At that moment we heard in the movie that Jesus said, "I'll be with you to the end of the world." I thought in my heart that He came for me.

All that month I couldn't forget the way He was talking to His disciples. In the kitchen while I warmed the water for tea, I thought, *He's talking to me and He's coming back. He will walk in our door*...I felt in these moments that He was right in front of me.

When the doctor's wife gave me the Bible, I didn't know where to start. So I started from the beginning and learned about the life of Joseph. I didn't know where the New Testament was or where the Old Testament was. So I read some, closed it up and put it away. After a week, she asked me, "Did you read the Bible?" I said, "Yeah, I read some, but I didn't like it." She asked, "Did you read the whole book?" I said, "No, I read about Joseph and Jacob and all that." Then she told me to open the book, and about halfway I could start from Matthew.

I really loved the Gospel of Matthew. Then I read John: "from the beginning was God." But I wasn't believing that Jesus was the Son of God. I was thinking the way I always heard: that God hasn't ever been born and God could not be the physical son of Joseph.

I covered my Bible with giftwrapping paper to hide it. Then every morning in the hour-and-a-half on the bus to the university, I opened it up and read it. I was in the back of the bus where all the women must ride. As we moved down the street, one of my friends sitting next to me asked, "What is this book you're reading?" I told her, "It's a book of prayer. Do you want me to pray for you?" They always happily replied, "Yes." They ask for prayer when they have examinations and other things. Also, during those weeks when I would have problems, I read the Bible.

The Jesus film had stuck in my mind and really got me thinking. I was trying not to pay attention to it, telling myself, *It's just a movie.* When I went to bed that night and other nights, I thought, *Well, He came, He went on the cross and came back, showed Himself to disciples, but what happened to Him then? Where is He?* I told myself again, *Forget about it. It was just a movie.* Then I really asked a lot of questions from my Christian friend. I was thinking that she's really trying to make me leave Islam and become a convert. That kind of shook me up. Only after I read from the Book of John, Chapter 1 did I really understand who Jesus is. Before I had thought that Mohammed is God on one side, Jesus is God on the other side, and Moses is on another side. All of these are around me and I am sitting right in the middle.

So, I had to choose one. Mohammed says how to reach God: Cover your hair, don't paint your nails, wear the robe, and wash yourself in certain ways. All of these things for my body. I'd listened to this all these years, but I didn't reach God. So I scratched that off.

Then I thought of the Jewish beliefs, but I said, "Well, those Jews also had all the rituals and were legalistic." I felt that wasn't really the right way. But I knew that with all these religious ways around me, I'm not going to come out empty-handed. I was studying and wasn't really a very simple person. I was determined to understand it. I didn't know about the relationship of God and the Son. One thing that impressed me about Jesus was if He's only a regular person, only called a disciple, He's still much different from the other Islamic messengers or imams.

One night while looking through the New Testament, I realized that Jesus' birth was from God and His death was from God. I read about Him, how good He is and how spiritual He is, His coming and going and His living. Then I thought to myself that Mohammed is from a worldly mother and father, just like me. At about 2:30 in the morning, in bed, I knew that Jesus Christ is God. Some voice told me in my heart, in my mind, *Jesus Christ is the only one, believe Him.*

Some voice told me in my heart, in my mind, Jesus Christ is the only one, believe Him.

I called my friend in the morning and asked her about the Trinity. She explained to me that just as water and ice and steam are all the same, these three are all the same. Muslims believe that Christians worship three separate gods. I tell my mother sometimes about the Trinity that all our bodies are full of different x's and y's, but they can work in me and out of me and all for me.

On Tuesdays and Thursdays, we went across the city to Dr. Alam's home and had fellowship with seven or eight Christians. I was always waiting expectantly for those days to come so I could go and ask them all my questions. I

An Iranian Bible study

marked my Bible during the week. The points that I understood I would mark with yellow pencil. For the ones that I had a question, I used another color. My father began to ask me, "Where do you go on Tuesdays?" I told him, "I go to tape some things from somebody else's television." I didn't want to tell him I was going to a Bible study. I didn't want to give him a shock and tell him I'm a Christian.

One Thursday my father asked, "Where are you going again?" I did not want to lie anymore so I asked Jesus to help me. Jesus, at that moment, gave me the answer to tell my father. I walked across the room and stood close to my father. I said, "I'm going to a prayer meeting." He looked up and said, "Well, pray for me, too, because I am expecting some business deals." He had a truck to take loads to different places and wanted me to pray so he would get more business, for somebody to call for the truck.

Now I had known the doctor's family for a year-and-a-half. My father had seen one of the videotapes. When my parents realized that I was really respecting Jesus and I began to talk about the cross, they really knew something was going on. I would hold hands with my mother and sisters. We would pray for my father to be healed of his drug addiction. They did not know how to pray. They would all bow their heads with me. I told them, "Jesus can heal him. I will ask Jesus, and whatever I say then you all say, 'Amen.'" They were all very respectful. We needed help.

Every time I came home from the Bible study, they would stop washing dishes or cleaning and say, "Well, what did you learn? Did you get so much today again?" I opened my cloth bag and showed them more Bible verses and my notes. And then we prayed in the living room some more.

I could do this only when my father was gone. I also made it look like I hadn't gone out of the house. When he walked back in, I wouldn't have on my street clothing (the black robe) but my own brightly colored clothing. He would think that I had been home all day.

Sometimes I would go to the kitchen and ask Mother to pray. She was cooking and was making some kind of a dish like a quiche. I told her about Jesus, how Jesus came to make us know who God is. My mother poured the eggs into the pan and said, "I know it. I know it." But she didn't

Who Is Jesus?

know it. I explained how there was this distance between God and us, and Jesus Christ came to be a bridge.

I have seen that painting that shows footprints on the sand when Jesus was walking with someone on the beach. When there was only one set of footprints, they asked, "Where are the other footprints?" and they said, "That's the time that Jesus carried us." I told all of this to Mama. I told her that when we have problems, Jesus carries us. Mother replied, "Is that right? It's very interesting." Then Mother looked at me and said, "I know that there is a power on us now. Our life is getting better."

At first when I went to the Bible study, she was irritated, saying, "On your days off, you stop helping me. You're leaving—why?" She was very mad. But a few weeks later, after we had started praying for my father, Mother came to my bed and shook me, waking me up and said, "Get up, get up. Don't be late for your class."

Every time I came home from Bible study, my mother was anxious and came out of the kitchen. "What's new?" She found out this is interesting stuff. She was listening and asking, "Did you pray for me or your dad, for my foot that is aching?" Then finally one morning she asked, "Can I go with you? I can come with you so I can pray for your school and entrance examination at the university." Mother began asking me about Jesus.

I gave my Christian friends a hard time to learn more from them about the Bible. One night at the Bible study, I began to cry, telling my new friends how different things in my life had been, how I've been all messed up. The final doubts completely left me, and I received Jesus Christ.

I didn't know at that time that after I received Jesus I needed to be baptized. One night I dreamed there was a big party. All the women wore nice dresses. I knew they were all Christians. There was a door, but I couldn't go through it. Some voice told me because I hadn't been baptized I could not enter. The next morning I told my friend about my dream.

So I was baptized in the tub of their house. Four of the Christian families were there, eight or nine people were all crowded in that little bathroom, and some had to look through the doorway. They all congratulated me, and they sang and started saying, "Hallelujah!"

Some of my prayers were answered. I now tell my family to trust in Jesus Christ and let Jesus' Spirit come into you. The Holy Spirit just takes over and you can see the difference. My sister, whenever she prays, prays in Jesus' name. My youngest sister says the same thing. Now we have three Bibles in our home, and we have been reading. We really love to read the simple tracts as well as the Bible. My father has read the new birth tract. He told me it's okay to go to the water and get baptized so we can wash away our sins. He knows baptism is only one time, that we don't get baptized every once in a while.

Mother asks me a lot of questions. She has read that by the law, we cannot reach God; it's not just by reading the laws and revelations and all the legalism. My friends at the university always want me to pray for them. The three friends see the cross on my chain, and they hurry across the courtyards and hold the little cross with their hands and say, "Pray for us," so that they get good grades. The cross doesn't show clearly because of my scarf.

I also pass out copies of the Lord's Prayer. I had somebody write it with good handwriting. People ask me for some consultation or some guidance. I tell them where I get my guidance—in the Bible. Little by little, I'm witnessing to them. All of us are on one row on the bus. I changed the cover again on my Bible and still take it to school in my bag.

I have to take a religious class, different courses on Islam, in the university. The class is usually quiet. You cannot talk to these religious teachers. You don't want to really talk so much. The teacher was talking about when Iran took over a lot of countries in the past and how Muslims attacked other countries. Centuries ago Muslims even invaded Iran.

I was sitting two rows from the back in this room of about 200 students. I put down my pen and raised my hand. The teacher, with his beard and robe, looked up at me and stopped. I asked, "Why did this happen, because Islam is not supposed to shed blood as a religion of peace? They are not to have bloody things, you know, the sword and everything." The teacher challenged me, "Where did you hear this?" And I said, "I heard it from a good man who was making a speech in one of the conferences."

Fanatical students, called *Hezbollahs*, give speeches around the university. We students debate many things out in the square. But these theology classes are compulsory, and everybody has to pass this otherwise they cannot graduate.

First, the teacher looked back at his notes and did not answer. Maybe he felt like I might be Christian or I might have some other things on my mind. When I asked this question, the other students turned to look at me. Some said, "Yeah, that's right." The teacher was also talking about killing the Christians in Isfahan, when the Islamic Arabs attacked Iran centuries ago, and they killed a lot of people.

I GO TO A COPY SHOP TO COPY A TRACT ABOUT JESUS CHRIST AND PASS THESE OUT AT MY SCHOOL.

In the classroom many students continued to mumble, talking about this. Then the teacher started banging on his desk with his fan saying, "Be quiet." He never answered my question; he only gave me a question. He didn't give me an answer. After this for a while, he did not give me a grade. I was so scared that he might report me to the police. At the time when I asked the question, I wasn't scared, but now, when I think about it, I get the shivers.

I have two friends, and for their birthdays I bought them each a cross. I also had a ring that I didn't like, so I took it to a jeweler to melt it and make two crosses out of it. I gave one to a child and one to this student friend of mine. Later on somebody gave me a gold cross. We have to be careful how we wear these.

66

I gave one of the Bibles to my aunt. I gave another Bible to the bus driver's assistant, the bus that takes us to school. When I climbed on the bus one morning, the bus driver's assistant told me, "I really enjoyed that book. It was wonderful."

I go to a copy shop to copy a tract about Jesus Christ and pass these out at my school. I was hoping the copy shop man would ask a question so I could witness to him. I haven't seen him lately. I'm going back to see him again to see what his reaction has been. He was very interested because he asked a couple questions. I know when I go there, he's going to ask some more questions.

To those Christians who may read my testimony, I would say, "According to your faith you can move mountains." There's no problem. Jesus says you will be healed by your faith, then you'll be healed. Jesus also is telling you, "Pray, pray, pray to get your victory."

I love the Bible verse, "I have been crucified with Jesus" (Galatians 2:20). And who lives in me, is not me anymore, it's Jesus. Jesus lives in me. Every time I say that verse, I cry. Jesus Christ became my father. I'm sure he's going to be sending a husband for me, a Christian husband. I tell God, "Save one for me." My mind has changed; my whole body and mind have changed so much that I don't want to really talk to an unbeliever as a boyfriend.

Now I am beginning to pray for Christians who are persecuted in other countries like in Iran. I also want to say a prayer for those women who don't know Jesus:

Father, I ask You and Your Son, Jesus Christ, I pray that they receive You as their personal Savior and open their hearts to You and themselves and fill up their neighbor's heart. And put love in the hearts of their husbands so they become believers. The same love that You put in my heart, in our hearts, from Jesus Christ, would start to be in the hearts of their husbands even when they persecute their wives. And day by day, You would add to their faith. Answer the prayers of their wives, Father. Amen.

WAITING *for the* PROMISED MAHDI

๑๛

Arman

E ach week I would ride five hours in a taxi to a mosque, almost 160 kilometers (100 miles) from where I live, looking for the Promised Mahdi. Muslims believe the prophet Mahdi will appear at the end of the days, even before Jesus. I was told that sometimes the prophet Mahdi appears and reveals himself to people at this mosque. But first you have to visit this mosque for almost ten months, for forty Tuesdays. There you bring your requests to him with the possibility that he might appear to you, talk to you, and grant your requests.

I went every Tuesday for almost ten months. The cost of the transportation is higher in certain seasons. But because I was so desperate to receive an answer from this prophet, I would ride two-and-a-half hours in a taxi to get there. I spent almost a year's salary just for transportation costs to and from this mosque.

The Promised Mahdi was a descendant of Mohammed. Syed Mohammed was born in India in 1443, and declared himself "The Promised Mahdi," who taught the true inner meaning of the Koran. He died of a fever at the age of sixty-three. Each Tuesday I would ride to the mosque and recite the prayers with all the washing and bowing. This ritual took almost two hours.

Before I came to know the Lord, one year and one month ago, I was as a dead person. I asked God, "God, I don't have any specific family in this world. Why did You make me be born?" I was born in the southern part of Tehran, where many smugglers, thieves, and drug addicts live.

I WAS SO DESPERATE TO RECEIVE AN ANSWER FROM THIS PROPHET, I SPENT ALMOST A YEAR'S SALARY JUST FOR TRANSPORTATION TO AND FROM THIS MOSQUE.

My family didn't worship much. They were nominal Muslims. At the age of six or seven, I realized there was no one who could really look after me, so I started working in the streets after school. I would sell sweets or things like that until I was in the sixth grade. Early in the morning, I would leave the house at 6 o'clock to spend two hours with some of my friends.

Later, I was involved in distributing some tapes of singers and selling CDs and illegal things that the government did not approve of. My friend had a shop, so people would come and buy things from me. I got a full-time job

70

as a tailor making clothes. A year after that, my mom passed away. She had loved me so much.

My dad and I couldn't really sit down and talk to each other face to face. He would give me a small amount of money every day, so that I wouldn't work in other illegal jobs. We would visit at home only once every two or three months. My dad didn't care for me.

From 8 o'clock in the morning until 8 or 9 in the evening, I would go to work as a tailor. Then I would go to my friends and we would stay together visiting until 2 or 3 o'clock in the morning. In my teen years, I began smoking cigarettes and having sexual relationships with young women. After a while, I did not enjoy that. I also caught an illness from that when I was age sixteen.

I flew to Kish Island, a free-trade zone of Iran, so that I could find a better job. On Kish Island, Muslims can get involved in all kinds of sins because the island is not geographically connected to the Iranian Islamic Republic. They are still building luxury hotels there. You can get what you want. I decided to give Dad a call. My dad told me, "Ali, you are no longer my son. Please don't come back home." He was so angry with me. He realized I had also stolen some money from him, and he was angry I had gone to Kish in a heathen way. I hadn't informed him, as I had gone in secret.

A week later, I called my older sister in Tehran. She was not at home, so I talked to her daughter who said, "Actually, everyone thinks that you are dead. We had a mourning service here for you because no one knew anything about you." My sister told me that Dad was not feeling well and was about to have a stroke. A day later, I called my father who got very emotional. He started crying and asked me to come back home. I had quite a good job on the island. I was a salesman in one of the clothes shops, and I was living in the house of the owner of that shop.

When I returned back home to find work in another tailor shop, they were happy and excited to see me, but I was full of regret. I thought maybe I shouldn't have come back. What does it mean to show love to one another?

When I was with my family, I would pretend to be someone very loving and caring, very kind and generous, but inside I had this feeling of hatred. All the bad feelings were struggling within me. I had hatred against everything. In the shop where I was working, I got to know two or three friends. They led me into using drugs. I felt that my life was being destroyed. I had the feeling God did not care about me at all. I was a dead person who was just moving.

Sometimes at home I would just sit and cry out to God, "God, I feel that even You have forgotten me, and there is no one caring about me. I really need to be saved, but I don't know how."

I realized I really had to decide to change. I had been attending traditional Muslim programs, mourning the prophets Hussein, Ali, or others who had died. I kept looking for a means to be saved. In desperation, this is when I began to search for the Promised Mahdi.

A Muslim said he had seen the prophet Mahdi in his dream. Mahdi told him, "Build a mosque for me so that people can come together here." In the beginning it was quite a small mosque, but during the years they have made it bigger. Basically this great mosque is way out in the middle of a desert. There is no city around it. The closest city is Qum. There is this belief that perhaps Mahdi himself comes to his mosque once a month to pray. There he prays for the people waiting and heals them and does some miracles for them.

When I would go on Tuesdays, there were great masses of people there. The mosque itself is not big enough for all these people so outside the mosque they have created a courtyard with long Iranian carpets, so many people can sit next to each other. I know 200,000 people would definitely be there, all looking for help. There is a day that is believed to be Mahdi's birthday. On that day more people come, even from other countries—India or nearby countries—all hoping for a revelation.

Behind the mosque is a well. People who have requests for Mahdi or some prayers write them on a piece of paper, along with a verse from the Koran, and throw the paper to the bottom of the well. They believe that at a certain time Mahdi comes and reads all these papers. Once or twice I wrote my request and put it in the well. But I still didn't get an answer. Maybe Mahdi didn't have time to read it.

Ten months of trips to Mahdi's mosque did not help me at all! It was useless spending all that money going there. When I came back, I realized that instead of receiving more peace, I got even worse and even more aggressive. I would even abuse my girlfriend.

But I could find no other way. I continued the long trips through the desert. If I knew the traffic would be heavy then, I would hurry in a taxi early in the morning to make sure I would be there on time. I still had this hope that the prophet Mahdi would appear to guide me, but there was no response. So I tried more relationships with girls. But it didn't help. I would feel so guilty, and there was even more pressure.

Then I reached a point in my life where I said, "There doesn't seem to be any God, otherwise He would have cared about me. I can do whatever I want. No one will care."

One afternoon I was with my second cousin, a musician, to get some chords and notes from him. We started talking about the problems we had regarding love. His older brother watching us said, "Did you go to the Mahdi mosque? Did you get any answers to your request?" I replied that it was useless.

My cousin told me, "Ali, you have been to all these different places to get answers, but have you really gotten anything out of it? I will introduce you to something better, but I really want you to keep it confidential. Don't tell anyone. Go to Jesus. He will answer your questions in the same way that He did for me."

I was quite impressed. I remembered when I was 8 to 10 years old and even later I had heard about Jesus. I had more love for Him than for the Islamic prophets.

In Islamic law if you want your prayers to be heard, you go to the mosque. I really wanted my prayers to Jesus to be heard. So that week I found a church building. It was an Armenian Orthodox church. I went and sat on the first row of the church. I quickly looked around. There were a few people scattered in the church that day. I really didn't know how to pray, so I just sat and folded my hands. Then I said, "Jesus, Mohammed is a father to me, but You are also an uncle to me. Sometimes my uncle cares more about me than my father. So Jesus, I want You to come and save me from this feeling of being lost, from my drug addiction and struggles. I really need Your peace to come to me."

"Go to Jesus. He will answer your questions in the same way that He did for me."

At the end of my prayer when I stood up to leave, I heard music as if Jesus was answering my prayers. Actually, someone was playing music in the church. I walked out the door feeling that God had answered my prayers. I went back to my cousin who had told me to go to Jesus. I told him, "Now I trust Mohammed is my father and Jesus is my uncle." He said, "No, Mohammed and other prophets are not really real prophets, but Jesus is. You should just ask forgiveness from Jesus because you have to repent from your sins."

On the way back home in the bus, I was thinking about the importance of forgiveness in my life. Finally inside our house, I raised my hands out to God and said, "God, I really want to repent if this is something that I have to do to please You. I am just going to repent of all

75

my sins, all the things that I have done. Jesus, if You are really the Lord, if You are the Son of God, please come and set me free." After that good time of prayer, I just got dressed to go out. I had the feeling everything had changed and I could feel a real freedom. I returned to my cousin to ask some questions.

I have heard that Islamic prophets have done some signs and miracles. My cousin said, "Even in the Word of God it says that there have been false prophets who have performed miracles and have led people astray, but you shouldn't be deceived by that." But I didn't have this Word of God, the Bible, that he was talking about.

I asked him, but he couldn't find one for me. So I decided to go look in different bookshops. There were none. I told God, "You showed me that I had to repent. But now You have got to give me Your Word as well." It was so important for me to have the Bible, no matter how expensive it would be. I went to a big square where there were many bookshops. At last I found a New Testament. I was so excited and started reading through it that night. Even as I got on the bus, I was reading it all the way back home. By the end of that evening, I had already read the Gospel of Matthew, Acts, and some of Romans. When I read the Gospel of Matthew, I had the feeling my faith had become complete. It was clear for me this was where my dependence had to be.

From the point I became a Christian until the time that I joined a cell group, there was a seven-month gap. The cell church sent a Christian boy from their group to come and visit me and strengthen me in my faith. I felt as if God had hugged me; I could feel the warmth of His hands around me.

The presence of Jesus filled in all the things that were lacking in my life. I was so enthusiastic to read and memorize the Word of God, even in buses and taxis!

I couldn't join a house church soon. This person from the cell group had been appointed to come and spend time with me so they could make sure I was not a spy pretending I was a Christian. Some false new converts go there to get information. In Iran, that happens.

I was twenty-four years old and basically alone. I prayed, "God, I really want to be with other Christians." God talked to my heart and said, "Your priority should be to seek My presence in your life at this stage. I am with you now, so I think your greatest need is met for now."

So I never insisted on really joining right away. Seven months later I was given the permission to go to the cell group.

Being with the brothers and sisters in the church replaced the lack of love I had in my life. In the cell church, they provided a very warm environment for me, so I could really share some of the hidden things that were in my heart. They encouraged me to carry on with my education, because I had left school. They even told me that whatever needs I had I could come to them. Also, if I had problems studying they were happy to help me with that as well. The brother in charge of our cell group asked me to go on evangelism trips to the cities, our mission field.

Due to competition, the tailor shop where I worked was not doing well. But the church had always been there to support me and encourage me. One of the ladies in our group encouraged me to take some courses to become a barber; now I am doing some training courses for that.

My younger sister knows I believe in Jesus. She doesn't take it that seriously. She tells me maybe I shouldn't have done it, but it is not a big issue for her because she herself does not have any belief in Islam. Each person has a different level of belief in Iran. Some believe many prophets. Others say, "This is the main prophet we believe in." You have got to know their boundaries.

My second cousin who told me about Jesus is about my age. I could trust him, and he could trust me as well. I could see the fruit of Jesus in his life, not just talk. I had heard there was this person called Jesus, considered a prophet in the Koran. As I grew older, I had the chance to visit some of the Armenian people. Many Armenians are nominal Christians, but I saw some Armenian Christians had a special love for one another. This really touched me a lot.

As a Muslim, the only thing I had heard about the Bible is the belief among some Muslim people that the "Bible" has been changed. They said if one word has been changed, it is not true. Some said, "How could the Bible be written, especially the Gospels—Matthew, Luke, John, and Mark?" When they look at it, they say, "If the Word of God is really divine, how could it be written by human beings?" So they said it has definitely been changed. Or maybe because there is no indication of their prophet, Mohammed, in the Bible, they disregard it.

Since the Bible Society was closed, you can't easily find a Bible. Some bookshops are hesitant to just sell one to you because it is not really safe to do it. We are trying to be quite wise. In my home I can't talk about the cell church. My younger sister doesn't have a strong belief in Islam, but she is quite concerned about what others think. She has to research about Jesus from her other friends. In this way the news spread in my family, among my other family members and my other sisters, that I had become a Christian.

IF YOU ARE A MUSLIM AND HAVE LEFT YOUR RELIGION, THEN . . . ANYONE CAN COME AND KILL YOU AND NOT BE JUDGED.

My other sisters are not happy about my conversion, especially two of them who are more fanatical Muslims. When they come to our house, I usually try to hide my Bible or Christian materials from them. If they see these things, they get angry. In Islam it is said that if you are a Muslim and have left your religion, then basically there is no protection for you whatsoever. Anyone can come and kill you and not be judged because you have become an infidel. My sisters are afraid someone will come and kill me.

If there were peace in Islam, I would not have come to Christianity. When I was a Muslim, I had all these lustful thoughts, I had hatred, and I was hypocritical and just trying to look good, but inside of me there were all of these horrible feelings and thoughts that I had. Now in Jesus I have a new heart. In jihad they are hateful and keep saying, "Death to America." This is just hypocritical because most of the goods coming into their countries are from America. So, I don't believe in that. The people involved in these issues are national leaders, families of those killed in the war against Iraq or military.

When you approach a Muslim family to witness to them, you can't talk about their prophet and then compare Jesus with him. You have to show in your actions that you are a Christian by the way you love them and build a friendship. Then share with them, and tell them, "For all your problems there is someone who can set you free. It is Jesus." I give them the gospel. Some of them open their hearts and share their problems.

I then ask them, "Okay, so why don't you go to God? Have you tried going to God?" Some of them say, "Well, we have done our prayers." I tell them, "Okay, why don't you approach God another way? Approach the heavenly God through Jesus." I tell them that through Jesus they can have access to God the Father. Those who are open to this are more curious and ask more questions. But those whose hearts aren't even close, just stop the conversation; they are not interested to go on. For those who are interested, I give them a New Testament, and tell them if they want to find out more about it then they can read it here.

When I personally share with people and talk about God and Jesus, I introduce Him as God the Father and Jesus as His only begotten Son. They never ask me whether we are talking about Allah or God. They feel I am introducing a new God to them. So, there has never been a question. We usually pray that God opens their minds so they will know they are confronted with the true God. I think it is true because it seems they are no longer interested in talking about the Muslim Allah when they come to Christianity.

I have learned that Allah is an idol. If he were someone real, he would be God of light, and we would experience him in our lives. He wouldn't be someone far away that we wouldn't have any access to.

For Muslims, Allah is someone quite far away, like a remote king sitting on his throne ruling over the people. Even if they want to take their request to Allah, it has to be in the name of one of these prophets—Ali, Hussein, or another. There has to be a mediator for them to take the request up. Basically, whatever I ask God in Jesus' name He really answers. When I asked Allah, there was no answer.

What I found really amazing was that in the Bible you read about the will of God, all the different ways God has talked through the people, all God's commandments to us, and many other passages that offer a personal relationship. I really don't want to judge Mohammed or Hussein or Ali and others because I am not sure what stage they were exactly in before they left this world. But I do not consider them as real prophets. I believe Mohammed and the other prophets lead Muslims astray from God, the real God.

My cousin said Jesus was born by the power of the Holy Spirit, and he kept asking me, "Who was the one who was really divine?" He said Jesus was incarnated and came to this world and did all these miracles. He asked questions to open my mind. You can't find all this truth in the Muslim prophets.

Muslim people sit down, they stand, and they bow. He told me that when you want to pray to God, you don't have to bow down. My cousin said, "You can just pray to God as you are standing. You can pray to God no matter what position you're in." He told me a lot about how to pray. He said, "When you go into God's presence, you shouldn't look at Him as someone who is very far away, because He is a loving Father. Speak as if He is next to you. You can open your heart to Him and just ask Him about the things that you need." My cousin has helped me to really understand the importance of my faith. You have to really ask God to remove all the chains that are still on your heart from the enemy and you need to be truly set free.

I SEE ON ONE HAND THE SUFFERINGS AND THE OTHER HAND A GLORIOUS HOPE.

Matthew 7:7 is my favorite Scripture passage: "Seek, and you will find; knock and it will be opened to you." Knock at the door. First Peter 1:16, "Be holy in the same way that I am holy," and 1 Timothy 4:12–16 about living with love, faith, and a pure life.

There are different activities in the cell church in Iran. We train people to go out for evangelistic ministries or sometimes through the Internet we chat with people. There are some people who are interested, and we get their numbers and then contact them. The cell church is growing in number as well as in kinds of activities that we do.

I believe at the same time God is protecting us, on the other hand, in the Word of God, we read that Satan is a roaring lion just standing around to come and grab us. I believe there will be some problems. Persecution may come, maybe from the government or from the families that are not Christians.

I basically try to grow more in His Word to prepare in case I am persecuted. I try to be encouraged more by the passages in the Bible where it talks about the suffering of Jesus because I realize Jesus did not go straight to the cross; He wasn't nailed on the cross so easily. He had to suffer a lot of hatred even before He was crucified. On the other hand, when I look at the glorious future that is ahead of us, that glorious hope we have, that is quite encouraging. I see on one hand the sufferings and the other hand a glorious hope.

I look at the Word as a source of blessing. I read different passages from the Bible not as a duty; I read them to receive a message from God. I try to memorize as many verses as I can. Some of our group will go to the Book of Psalms and each one of us will memorize one of the chapters in order to learn the Word of God by heart.

We gather at times in groups of a hundred people, but usually we have ten to twenty meeting in a house. There are drinks and snacks on the table. We sing and maybe use our musical instruments for the bigger groups.

We really pray a lot before we witness to people. People get angry at us. It hasn't happened to me so far. I really pray God guides me as I evangelize and I pray God puts it in my heart if it is not the right time to talk. He guides me. Ninety percent of the cases when I share with people about Jesus, they are really open to the message. They are so interested, which is a good beginning.

NINETY PERCENT OF THE CASES WHEN I SHARE WITH PEOPLE ABOUT JESUS, THEY ARE REALLY OPEN TO THE MESSAGE.

Our cell groups can't really sing songs with a loud voice because we are afraid it might cause problems for us. We just hope we can come together and freely worship God without being concerned about all the noises that might disturb the neighbors.

When you pray for Iran, you can say, "God, I am praying for a country that is still bound by the spirit of Law under Shariah and all their Islamic rules and regulations."

Pray for the Christians who are saved in Iran:

God, You give them the special wisdom they need, that they know how to approach these people who are so bound by Islamic laws. Lord, I pray You remove all these obstacles in the way of the Christians there who are caught by attacks of the enemy, the ridicule from their families. Soften the hearts of those who are quite hard against the message of the gospel, so that they can be open and accept it. Fill them with Your Spirit, and then guide them for Your own glory. Give Your divine peace to Your children. My prayer is that there will be a day when all these Christians having to meet as underground churches can worship You as the only God all together, not in different groups of underground churches.

Without Jesus in my life, I would be dead. Before I knew Him, a few times it crossed my mind to commit suicide. I would carry a razor just to try to harm myself. But I couldn't do it. I would just use a sharp thing to cut a line in my hand. I know if I didn't have Jesus in my life, maybe I would physically be alive, but my inner life would be dead.

I am hoping I learn the Word very well, so that I can teach it. I would like someday to be a teacher of the Word of God. Once, when I was praying asking God to give me the right gift, I had the feeling as if God wants to give me the gift of teaching. Then I talked to my pastor and he was in agreement that I have the potential and ability to teach others. So I feel this is where God is calling me. I really thank God, I now see that I have so many millions of sisters and brothers in the world.

TWO LIGHTS
in the DESERT

🜪

Dr. and Bita G.

Dr. G.

I practice medicine. When the Iranian government learned I was not a faithful Muslim, they sent me way into the desert wilderness to work in a little clinic. They thought this would muzzle my faith in Christ, shut me up. They forgot one thing: I work with people, not with rocks. People are looking for love, for hope.

When I was seven years old, I looked up on the mantle and saw the Koran. I asked my family why it was on the mantle and no one was reading it. No one answered my questions. Not many read it. It is a symbol. They tell the children in Iran that they are born Muslim and have to stay Muslim. I didn't accept what they were telling me, so at eight years old, I began to learn the Koran. I started praying every day and followed all the Muslim rituals. At nine,

I completely knew about the Koran and rituals of Islam. I had my own gold-colored silk prayer rug and the handkerchief where I folded my beads and other religious items. Somebody had brought these as gifts from Mecca. Our finances were not real good. We didn't have much furniture, so we had to store many things under our beds. But I always carefully folded my rug and handkerchief and put them on the mantle by the Koran.

As a young boy of ten or eleven years old, as I would walk to school, I would pass a church and look up at it. I was attracted to that building. One of my friends at that time, an Armenian, took me to his home, and I saw the Bible for the first time.

It is not permitted to question or to "research" the words of the Koran.

He asked, "Would you like to have one?" And I said, "Yes, I like to study, and this will give me something to read." A few days later, he handed me a Gospel of Matthew. The paper was so old that it was brown and fragile. This was before the Islamic revolution. I still have that book.

In high school I asked my teachers lots of religious questions. They tried to avoid these. Later, I realized they couldn't get too close to the depth of this material, because they could drown in it and not find their way out. Also, it is not permitted to question or to "research" the words of the Koran.

I had an Islamic theology teacher who was dressed like a typical mullah. He wore a black robe, a black turban, and had a long black beard. He was fifty-six years old. He had studied in Qum for thirty years, a holy Muslim city in Iran. He carried green beads. Green is the holy color, a sign that he is from a religious family, a descendant of Mohammed. He said, "I can't give you the answer," or "Well, just don't bother too much about it." The Ayatollah Khomeini's sons became Communists when nobody gave them the answers. They were killed because they were searching for the truth.

I discovered in our sacred writings where it is written that we should not wear black. I asked them why the women all wear black. Many of our rituals and chants originated not from Mohammed, but from a king of the Sabaeans who wrote twelve books about Islam. Many young people, like myself, were trying to find the truth.

I had lost much of my family in the Iran-Iraq war. My mother and father were killed when I was fourteen years old. Saddam was sending his scud missiles and bombs to destroy the refinery. One brother and one sister were also killed when Saddam bombed our city.

I was left with two sisters and another brother. We had been in another city visiting relatives. I hated the Iraqis who killed my family.

I started studying Baha'i and other religious sects to see who is telling the truth. I wanted to choose the best religion—Jewish, Christian, or Zoroastrian. I used to buy books or go to the library at the university. I still have some of them in my bookcases.

There were religious wars in Europe for many years between Christianity and Islam. But in Iran, under our new

(1979) Islamic regime, it took only twenty years for our own people to become sick of Islam. Little by little, they started leaving it, and now only about 10 percent are following it. All the rest are searching.

When I was sixteen years old, I met a Christian named Nader in a café—a teahouse. He saw me sitting alone, angry about life. He began to make friends with me, asking what's the matter with me. That day, I'd had an argument about my grade with one of my teachers. I was mad and kind of depressed, drinking tea when he came up to me.

He asked me in a kind way, "May I sit next to you?" I said, "Yes," but I didn't trust him. He scooted his chair up and asked me, "May I help you?" I didn't want to talk. I shot back, "Are you my teacher to help me?" He learned I had an argument with my teacher. After we visited in this noisy place a while, I asked, "Can you give me a telephone number or anything so I can reach you again?" He said, "I haven't got a number yet." I told him, "I'm living upstairs with my sisters in an apartment. You're welcome to come see me anytime you want to."

Six months later Nader called and asked me to come to the same café. He said, "I don't want anyone on campus to see us together. It might cause you problems, especially for your education." Many students already didn't like me because I'd talk to them about religions and sects and even about the Hezbollah radicals. Some students who were searching would ask me questions. But a Hezbollah radical had spotted me with Nader and confronted me, "Why are you associating with this guy and these Christian people?"

Now when I look back at this, I am grateful Jesus said, "I came for the sick, not for the healthy." I remember the time a lady went to wash Jesus' feet with her hair and with oil, and Jesus said, "She's more blessed than you people here that brought Me to your table." I have learned from Nader that we have to minister to everybody.

Nader still didn't open up to me with what he had in mind. He always talked about God—you've got to know God, the real God. But he didn't yet really tell me who the real God is. He made me eager to know more. First, he gave me some tracts. He didn't give me a Bible or any books. Later on, Nader told me he would have some more Gospel books for me, knowing I had read the Gospel of Matthew, but then he disappeared. I never saw him again.

One morning I went to visit my fiancée's parents about plans to marry their daughter. There in the living room, I met a visitor to the family—Mr. Bazargan, a Christian. I was surprised. Mr. Bazargan told me about the truth and about God. I told him about my past.

He said, "Well, you don't have any mother and father; I will take you in as a son. And I'll be happy to help you." The spark that first came to my heart from Nader now spread as I learned about God and read about Jesus in the Bible.

As we sat at the table with lots of fruit, some dried apricots, and pistachio nuts before us, we had a good time. The steaming teapot was set before us. I told Mr. Bazargan that I was interested to learn more about Jesus, who He is and what He's done. So he brought me some simple books in Farsi and some tapes, preaching and teaching, from overseas. I started reading the books.

Back at home, when no one was around, I would duplicate these tapes and give them to my future wife and other people. During this time, I learned who Jesus is, and I accepted Him as my personal Savior.

> *THOSE OTHER RELIGIONS . . . ALL EXPLOITED OUR DESIRE FOR GOD, BUT THEY DIDN'T TELL US ABOUT A RELATIONSHIP WITH GOD.*

I found out that many of those other religions influence you to control you for their personal gain. They all exploited our desire for God, but they didn't tell us about a relationship with God. Islam was saying you have to go through the prophets to go to Allah or their god. The Zoroastrians also have a book based on good deeds, worshiping earth, water, wind, and fire.

Good deeds, good thoughts, good acts. But when I read material about Christianity, I discovered that we can go immediately to God. I found out that's the only way to go to God and know God. You have to go straight to God through Jesus and not go through other people. Another guy gave me an example; he said, "It's just like you want to borrow some money. You don't tell another person to come tell me you want to borrow some money. You come straight to me to borrow the money, because the other guy might deceive you."

The second year I was a Christian, I told my wife about my decision to follow Christ. She was a very devoted Muslim and prayed every day. But I didn't stop her from doing it and still kept loving her. I knew I had to be a good witness to her. Once she quietly said, "Give me some time, I'll come around."

I was baptized with others two years later in Mr. Bazargan's house bathtub, and dedicated my life to the Lord. My wife was there. We sang some songs. I was so relieved and felt like I could fly. We sang a song about all the angels clapping in the sky. My wife was baptized a short time later.

Bita

Nobody can say they don't believe in anything or anybody. There is always somebody people believe in. I was traditionally Muslim, following my family, praying five times a day and fasting at Ramadan. I went through all the Muslim rituals at home and didn't go to the mosque on Fridays, but a lot of women went. I did my rituals at home. While I was doing all the rituals, I was thinking something was missing. We were living in an oil-producing city in southern Iran. After I graduated from high school, we moved. All this time, I was still searching. I became acquainted with Dr. G. and we got married. I knew that he was a Christian, but I just wanted to marry him. He gave me a Bible. After I read the Bible, I knew the missing connection was right there.

My parents didn't know he was a Christian when I married him. (Even though he hadn't told me he was a Christian, I knew.) But they were very open-minded. They said if that's what's going to make me happy, go be happy.

In Iran, many women who wear the long black robes have short skirts, bright colors, short-sleeve shirts, and anything to be colorfully different under their robes. This shows Islam is a manmade oppression—not something spiritual from the heart.

I read a little book, *Knowing God*, which gave me great certainty. "You can do whatever you want to do, and you can do or practice and be a great disciple for Me and witness for Me." That book helped me understand that all of this is real. I read the New Testament many times before I was baptized.

Now whenever I feel bad, the only book I go to is the Bible. Like the Bible says, there are many people who've said, "Jesus, Jesus, Jesus," but they don't know really who Jesus is. I give these people books and Bible tracts. They learn so fast. They're searching, hungry, and they really receive the Word.

You have to be very careful Satan doesn't come around with pride and tell you that you really know all about it. He can make you have a big head. I ministered to a person, gave him a Bible and tracts, and told him to watch out for Satan, who interferes with your work and tells you that you know everything now and you don't need to learn any more. But we just can't tell them; they have to learn to keep Satan away.

My daughter is eleven years old. She's really on fire for the Lord. She must go to our schools that are Islamic, and she comes home with some confusion. Then we have to share truth with her and help her understand. At school they have ritual pictures on the wall and have to pray to Allah in ritual prayers. They have to read the Koran in class. It is all fanaticism. Every day as she walks to school, I am praying for her and on her way back home as well. If she has a test that day in school she says, "Mommy, Mommy, pray for me. I have a religious test in school. Pray to Jesus."

Our children have to read the Koran and another religious book to get good grades. If they don't get good grades in Koran and the religious books, no matter how good a grade they get on the other subjects, they flunk. They will not pass the year.

Dr. G.

One day my six-year-old son came home and said that his teacher asked him to go to one of his personal religious ritual ceremonies. My son told her, "No, because those people are thieves." So the authorities called me to the school office the next day. Especially since I am a man, I first have to knock at the office door. I heard a word inside, "*Y'Allah*" to let me come in. The principal wore a scarf and the black robe—chador. She had her face and everything covered to be decent. I sat down, and she ordered tea for me. The principal likes me because I'm a medical doctor and give her prescriptions and don't charge her anything. On her metal desk, there were some books, pens, pencils, and the flag of the Islamic Republic. A fan was making some noise. A window was open to the yard. This school building was a little house. It was a private school, but Islam is taught in public and private schools. We have no choice.

The principal said, "Why is this boy calling these people who go to the ceremony 'thieves'?" I explained to her that when people come to some of these rituals, they are asked to take a dish home from the event, a saucer or cup, as a souvenir of blessing. When they receive their blessing, they are supposed to bring six more cups or saucers back, removing more dishes from their homes. My son saw this as religious thievery. She seemed to understand. Later that afternoon when I got home, I told my son to be careful.

Our children have watched the movie of the life of Jesus Christ many times, even our six-year-old. They are young, so it can be dangerous. We try to tell them, "Don't tell any other people outside what we do at home, what we have been watching." We also tell them not to tell in school what you're doing at home, who comes to visit or who goes. "If you tell, somebody in school may be a spy. They will go tell the police, and then they will come arrest us and take us to jail. You don't want that to happen to your mother and dad." So they're more cautious now in public about our Christian activities at home.

Bita

The night after I was baptized in a bathtub, my house felt dark. Everything was so dark to me. But then I said, "In the name of Jesus, get away from me." And everything was gone. It was Satan trying to hold on to me, but when I said the name of Jesus, then everything became light. I was released and so joyful. I was so happy to be baptized. I knew if I got baptized, I'd be a different person like a new birth; and the old things would pass away, all the sins and bad things and I'm all new. Then we wanted to renew our marriage vows. Earlier we were married in the Islamic tradition, but after we were both baptized, we wanted to get married in the Christian tradition.

Dr. G.

We also knew that after we got baptized we would have a lot of problems. I wasn't getting employed anywhere. For seven years after getting my medical degree, no one gave me a job because I was a Christian. Even after I got a job, I was exiled to some little tiny villages.

I wasn't surprised. Before baptism, I knew the Christian life was about sacrifice and that baptism was a symbol of giving up our old life for Jesus. I knew when I became a Christian, I was about to go to jail, I was going to get beat up, and I was going to be persecuted. I was going to have a really bad time and might even get killed.

The first person who told me about fearing persecution was the first Christian I met years ago in the tea shop, Nader. He told me I might get persecuted, beat up, and jailed. From the beginning I knew I was stuck in a place where I was going to have problems. Even before I was a Christian, the first book Nader gave me was the Gospel of Matthew. All of Chapter 10 is about persecution. Jesus said they will beat you, they will arrest you. And after that, I read the Book of Acts about how much I should be prepared to go through persecution. The more I grew as a Christian, the more I knew I was susceptible to be persecuted.

Bita

But persecution is Jesus' way. If you follow Jesus, it is actually Him being persecuted. Yet He is our joy and pleasure. I bought a lot of Christian books, fifteen to twenty, in a big cloth sack and stopped by my aunt's house to talk to her a minute. She saw my bag and said, "Don't you take these books around town because the police will search you and take you to jail." She was so worried about me. Later, when I got home, our phone rang, and it was my aunt. "Did you get home safe?" she asked. I am careful, but I leave all of this in God's hands. Happy are those who follow Jesus; no matter what happens, they are victorious.

I tell others God loves us. It's Satan who wants to destroy us. You have cast Satan away from you when you know Jesus Christ's love. Jesus wants us to love Him like He loves us. God's hand, His shadow, is on us. He never leaves us. God is beautiful. I love the beauty of God.

Dr. G.

I knew I had to go to work for Jesus. My first "fish" was my wife, Bita, and I caught the fish. I gave her a book and said, "Read this. It will tell you who you should become in Christ." She became a Christian partner to help carry the load of our witness. I give Bibles to others even when this causes them to have problems because this is not the end of life. It's the beginning of life and the life beyond. I'll follow the way that I have chosen. I'm ready to pay the price.

I studied medicine for seven years. They would have kicked me out of the university in my medical studies if they knew I was a Christian. We still write "Muslim" on all our documents but continue to work for Christ secretly and openly. We know where our heart is. On the application to go get a passport, to travel outside Iran, where it states your religion, we write "Muslim." Those who follow the Baha'i religion are never given a passport. You have to say "Islam" or "Muslim" to get a passport.

Although some Armenians in Iran have legally stayed Christians, in my opinion, there are more Muslim-convert Christians now than Armenian Christians. There are now a lot of underground Muslim-convert Christians. It's very hard to tell how many, but Christianity is growing here. There are six churches allowed of different non-Muslim sects—Catholic, Assyrian, Armenian, and others—but only a few buildings where they can worship in all of Iran. Most are not evangelizing because of the danger. Some have even stopped helping little prayer groups of Muslim converts they started.

> PERSECUTION IS JESUS' WAY. IF YOU FOLLOW JESUS, IT IS ACTUALLY HIM BEING PERSECUTED.

Most of the young people right now are searching. They are waiting for somebody to reach them to receive the Lord. There are some good signs the people are changing. They don't tell each other openly, "I'm a Christian." But something is going on. One of the reasons is Christian books. We get 3,000 to 4,000 at a time, but they cannot be legally printed.

A few books are sold publicly, written by Muslims, with bits in them saying something about Christianity. This is done by the Islamic printing department. So many people are reading these books that you have to go to the street to find them, because you can't find them anymore in bookstores. Whenever Jesus' name is in a book, people look for it because they want to know about Jesus. Since they don't know anything about Jesus, they don't know if the book is biased or not. Before I had a Bible, when I was searching for these books, the shop owners were asking me, "Why are so many people coming after these books?" One small Christian book printed illegally is *The Part of the Praying Wife*. I don't think they can stop Christians from doing work.

If Muslim converts like us go into a church, we usually cannot sit in the pews and listen to what they're saying. We look different from the Armenians. Because of my darker face, they know I am from a Muslim background. Sometimes, afraid of persecution from the authorities, churches don't let us sit down. We can go in as a tourist to look around in some church buildings, but we have to leave. In Iran, our society thinks only Armenians are Christians, because of the cultural history, but only a tiny group in Iran is Armenian.

Once I went into a church. The pastor came to me and said kindly, "Well, we'll talk later after church, but not here." That was wise. The Islamic officials know more people are coming to Christianity. They have put pressure on the churches telling them not to encourage it. Many curious Muslims never go to church because they're so afraid of the state. Also, in almost all churches, the sermons are in the Armenian language. We don't understand what they say. One pastor told me, "They have told us not to preach in Farsi. We would like to preach in Farsi to get more people coming, but we are not supposed to." The government forces most churches to speak only in Armenian, not the national language of Farsi, so we Muslim-background believers are left in the dark. This is another way of keeping Muslims from going to church.

After graduation, I had two years of compulsory military service and then two years of medical social service. Wherever I work, I give Bibles, tracts, and cassettes to the patients from a briefcase when no one is looking. Some are younger generations of Armenians. They are all thirsty for the Word and don't have Bibles. They ask for them. They really want to become believers. They knew I was Christian and just wanted to come see me and talk about Christianity, but they had to get a medical report from my office for the secretary. I would state, "This patient doesn't need any medicine, he needs rest."

I was giving videos on the life of Jesus to the nurses out there. One nurse would watch it and tell another nurse, "The doctor has a good tape. You need to get it and watch it." They thought this was the only tape I had. But I told them, "I have many at home." They stopped by my desk and asked questions. When I saw their desire to know more, I said, "I have books you can read if you want. I can bring you one, but it's up to you to become a Christian or not." This gives me the chance to give them a Bible.

Every few days the state Islamic spy would call me into his office in the hospital where I worked. "Why are you not following Islamic rules?" It was just like they did to me in the army. I was spreading the gospel, so they continued to give me a hard time. "Why are you wearing short-sleeve shirts? You're supposed to wear long-sleeve shirts. Why are you using a razor? You're not supposed to use a razor according to Islam. Why do you shave?"

My office was on the first floor, across from the office of the hospital director. Religious intelligence would send a special person to go see how I was doing in that clinic. The man walked across the building to the clinic to watch my behavior. Every day he would take a report to headquarters. Frequently the watchman's secretary called me on the phone and said, "Mr. Hami wants to see you today."

I would go sit there in his big office with the file cabinets. The watchman had a beard and held the Muslim prayer beads in his hands. There were pictures of the ayatollahs on his wall, Khatami, Khomeini, and others above his head. These people interrogate you so much you're really scared when they call you into that office. In this location they called me four times. They wanted me to be an informer, and I refused. They wanted my sleeves long and wanted me to please them. They wanted me to tell if my coworkers were talking against the government or for the government, or having immoral relationships with a nurse or not, or stealing or not coming to work on time, but I refused. Finally, the last time I went in, he terminated my medical practice there.

I asked, "Why are you canceling my contract?" He said, "Because the interrogation department has said we don't need you." I asked him if he'd seen something wrong from me. He said, "No, but since we didn't see any good stuff in your file that makes us happy, we don't need you. We're going to cancel your contract." They kicked me out.

Now I was kicked out from another place, but many had found the Lord. Then the authorities wanted to isolate me even more and sent me to another town 160 kilometers (100 miles) away. They made me drive way out of town for four years to an isolated clinic because I refused to grow a beard, wear clothing like theirs, and be an informer. About 300 people came to my clinic each month, even in the desert area. Every day I drove the 160 kilometers back and forth. I had to get up at 6:00 in the morning, drive outside the city and across the desert, to get there on time. The authorities thought they were punishing me, but Jesus used me to reach new people.

It was a time for courage. My family had been killed in the Iran-Iraq war. All the people in Iran who have families with both mother and father killed in the war have privileges. They can get any job without any application but not our family. During the three years I was banned from medical work, I was helping remodel houses and selling appliances. I held on thinking, *You are passing through a test. You are going through trials and tribulations.* This made me patient as I painted, hammered, and carried materials, waiting to see what the Lord had in mind. I was becoming a stronger believer.

I had read about Jesus Christ and watched the movie about how much He took for me. I knew what I was taking wasn't anything like what Jesus took. Jesus showed me we have to be prepared. When you take up your cross, problems and troubles come your way. Be ready for it. You're going to have problems, worldly problems, but inside you will have peace, His peace.

God says, "I am your banner. In the hard times, I'm carrying you. And I'm always next to you, walking with you." God says, "When I come into your life, I never leave you nor forsake you."

While installing those washing machines and things having nothing to do with my medical practice, I was happy. I was still witnessing for the Lord. I was still giving the Bible to people and tracts to the people and sharing my happiness with them.

Finally, after three years out of medical work, I got a temporary position. I write prescriptions, do stitches when people cut their hands, care for emergencies, and give them some medicine. They pay a little bit for the medicine, as nothing is free. I check the children. There is a lot of diarrhea. I could make more money if I worked in my specialized field, but I am not allowed.

Bita

Some people ask us how we see God. "How do you know God? How do you receive God? Who is God in your life?" I tell them, "There's a God who always comes to my rescue, even my life. Our financial income is so little, like a hair, just like a strand of hair, but it won't fall off. God comes back and gives us many more blessings."

I tell them, "When I follow Jesus, I'm not worrying about our finances. I'm not worrying about getting persecuted. I'm not worrying about not having enough, because my God will supply all my needs. No matter what we go through, we're working for Him. He's going to reward us and bless us. Why don't you try Him, see what you think?"

> WHEN YOU TAKE UP YOUR CROSS, PROBLEMS AND TROUBLES COME YOUR WAY. BE READY FOR IT.

I tell them, "We don't have much, but we eat good, our appearance is nice and clean. We have a smile on our face and joy in our hearts." They ask us, "With all the things you are going through, how can you be so happy?" We say, "Because we have Jesus." This opens the doors.

I ask them, "You read in your Koran that Jesus Christ raised the dead. In another part of the Koran, it says, 'Whoever raised the dead is God.'[3] So you see, Jesus Christ is God, and you should believe in Him. According to the Koran, He is God." This opens the door as we start witnessing to them.

Dr. G.

After witnessing one-on-one for a few months, we started having a home Bible study. Sometimes we go outside of town to a private fruit orchard where it is quiet and no one can see us. Among the apples and pears and melons in the orchard, we start singing and have Bible study. On Friday early in the morning, we drive out of town and come home in the evening. Our relatives own this private orchard. We spread out our blankets, as it can be chilly in the morning. At noon, in the spring, we will take off our sweaters and hang them on the limbs. We will pour some *doogh* in cups, a yogurt drink, diluted with water. We put a little salt or mint in it sometimes.

Someone brings fruit in a bag, dates, or some nuts like almonds. In season we cut a watermelon and pass it around. The children play with a ball or other games while somebody watches them. While we're arranging this church picnic, we ask the individuals what happened last week, what did you do, who did you witness to, who did you see, and what did you give to the people? We get an activity report from each one of them.

We pass out song sheets and sing together. Sometimes someone will sing a solo, as we can't play musical instruments. If somebody heard that outside the garden, they would be curious and think we're having a party. The snoopers would run over and dismantle us, you know, interrupt us or maybe take us to jail. At our meetings we learn where some of us were interrogated in past weeks or if there were objections anywhere on the way. We report how many people we witnessed to or gave Bibles or tracts to. We are under the trees and share what the needs are. If there is a special need, we stop and pray for them first. If we can help their needs in any way, we would go back to town and try to help them.

If at the picnic worship we brought a new person to witness to, we would all be very careful and watch what we say. Then little by little, we would start witnessing to them. Sometimes if we did not have to work the next day, we would rest and play and have fellowship until the evening. I would teach most of the time from the Bible. Many in our group are new believers. But they're learning and coming along. When the sun is setting, we pack up and start back to town.

In the city more people are suspicious. Now I have to change our apartment again and move out. The landlord asks us, "Who are these visitors? What are they doing here?" I tell him, "They're my friends." But he comes back again, knocking on my door, and asking more questions, "Where are they from?"

I had a large sticker, "Hallelujah," on the back window of my car. This was the first time the police called me to their office. When I walked in, one of them asked, "What is this sign on the back of your car?" I replied, "It says, 'Thank you, God.'" He still wasn't happy. "Why don't you write it in Farsi?" I said, "That word would be too long for my window, so I stuck up the short version."

Even though my apartment was on a side street, evidently they had been watching my "Hallelujah" car for a while. I told them, "I'm going to sell my car, so why should I scrape it off?" It wasn't a lie. The car wasn't really running well after commuting for years out in the desert, so I sold it later. Everybody knew that car, so I had to do something.

I got another car. I still go out to share about Jesus. In a village where I witness sometimes, I give the video about Jesus to the people. The police heard about it. One evening two policemen knocked on my door. One held up a video. I don't know how he got it. He said, "What is this tape you're giving to the people?" My wife and children stayed back in the kitchen. I told them, "Well, you can find it anywhere. I'm not the only one giving it away. There are so many people who have these and are giving them away." As they turned to walk back down the stairs, one threatened, "Don't give these away anymore."

Even before I was baptized and working in the villages, the police would harass me. With their first phone call, a voice said, "We'd like to get some information from you. You need to come and present your information at our office." So I went there. It was near my home.

The police station looks like a fort. It has tall walls. On top of the walls, they have barbed wire like a prison. There are four towers, and all around there are guns. First, I called at the gate. They asked me to come in. I heard another officer inside tell them that I was there. He shouted across the inner yard, "Okay, I'm going to send somebody over to bring you in." They walked me in and put a blindfold on me. This station is a torture building. They take people in there and torture them. Sometimes they go in and never come out. The first time I went there, I didn't tell my wife because I didn't want her to worry. But the second time I told her, so she could pray for me.

In this two-story building, there is the basement where all the torture is going on. Upstairs is where they do the interrogations. Even with the blindfold, I knew they were taking me all the way down. We walked to a room, which I saw later only had one door. No windows, no light. They said, "Sit down." Then a man behind me pulled off the blindfold. They shined a big light in my eyes, so I wouldn't see who was interrogating me. A man behind the light said, "Tell the truth, we'll help you out. What are you doing? Tell us, and we will help you not to be on the bad list. We see some suspicious people come and go to your office and ask for you especially. There are also some Afghani and some Armenian people. Tell us what's going on." I got a little angry at them and said, "Whoever comes to me, it's because I'm a doctor. They need help."

Most of the questions were about the video tape of Jesus that I had been distributing. I said, "You can find that anywhere. I'm not the only one. A lot of people in town have it." So they asked, "Where did you get that tape?" I said, "Like anything else, I bought it out on the street. They're selling playing cards, they're selling alcohol, they're selling all kinds of bad videos, good videos. All the video stores have these. I can buy this stuff from the right people in the market. And you can go buy them, too."

(The other year when they brought the film *The Passion of the Christ*, people in Iran really wanted to see it.

A lot of people made a copy of the movie, duplicated it, and sold them in the market.)

The two policemen were asking me one question right after another to kind of throw me off. I couldn't see them, as the light was so strong in my face. They didn't put the handcuffs on me. This means you're not going to be released. But for an hour-and-a-half, the same question was repeated. In between they put common, ordinary questions to make me feel good. Then they came back to the movie. They played with my mind. One of them acted sympathetic. "Everybody is having a hard time, you know. It's such a bad time, these years in Iran. Everybody is suffering," one said. Then the other said, "How many were there at that meeting you set?" They were trying to tire me out, wear me down. They finished with a command: "Don't do this anymore. If we catch you again, you're going to have a hard time."

They put the blindfold back on me and led me to the door. One said, "Sorry, it was a misunderstanding." I didn't go directly home because I was kind of shaky. I walked around for a while then sat on a stone wall by the river to get relaxed before I went home.

The first time I told my wife about the police, she cried a lot. She was so scared. Our little girl was four years old. I don't want to remember that day, it was so fearful. I had a

WE'RE ALWAYS READY TO GO TO OUR MAIN HOME WITH JESUS. I'M NOT AFRAID OF DEATH BECAUSE I KNOW WHERE I'M GOING.

hard time. I told her they might control the telephone conversations, so we started to talk about our church members using code words. We would not say "Christian," "brother," "sister," or "meeting" on the phone, but we used other words.

The Security Office in Iran *(Verzarat e Etelatt)* is so strong, more than ever before. If the police want somebody's biography, they can have it in a short time—who our mother was, our father was, all of our relatives. They have a good file on me. We have to be aware that there's a mouse in the wall, a bug planted, so they can hear us. We are careful of our telephone calls.

A third time, the police called me on the phone. They said, "You smell like a convert." I said, "No, I'm not proven" (meaning not yet baptized). They said, "If this is proven, you are dead."

We must move every two or three years. We have moved six times so far. This is the seventh place we've moved to in thirteen years, yet this is not important. We don't want any home here because we know where our home is. We're always ready to go to our main home with Jesus. I'm not afraid of death because I know where I'm going. John 3:16 tells our family when you believe and seek Jesus, you have abundant life. You have everlasting life. Jesus said, "I am the way and the truth and the life."

Our meetings change around because we do not want to be caught, to be stopped. Sometimes we have them once a week or sometimes once a month. When we know that they are following us, we may have our large meeting once in two months. We call each other and tell each other what's going on. The other month, because of some kind of a crackdown when a lot of people were going to rise up against the government, the police in our city were standing at every corner of the streets with machine guns. Nobody can move or do any wrong things. We didn't get together that month but met only with our family. We get together at 10:00 or 11:00 at night, coming up the stairs one by one.

> WHEN PEOPLE ACCEPT JESUS CHRIST AND FOLLOW ALL HIS COMMANDMENTS, ... THEY KNOW HIS PROMISE THAT DEATH IS NOT THE END OF EVERYTHING.

When there's a new tape, audio or video, that we have received, we play it and then we copy it for others. No Bibles are printed in Iran, but we all have a Bible. I continue to teach systematically from the beginning of the New Testament. We sit in a circle on the floor and each read the verses. Everybody reads a verse or two. This way everybody has a review of the lesson. One or two persons really listen, and they review the verses. We keep a verse in our heart when we go out into the world.

There are a lot of religions with an imaginary god, and they don't know who God is. They worship it for nothing. We know who Jesus is. He's proven that He's God. He lived among us. Jesus is the real God. I'm following the same God I believe now. I don't go just to the right or left. I know the way I'm going, and I'm just following through.

I'm not going to get under the influence of my feelings. I don't sacrifice the truth for the worldly things or feelings or let them change my way of life.

Although there are interrogations and warnings, we have an expression in Farsi: "When you are drowning, it doesn't matter how much the water goes up, one inch or one meter." So, when you go to prison, then you just forget all your fears.

Living in Iran, my security is in Jesus Christ. When people accept Jesus Christ and follow all His commandments, without gaining some personal interest, but just walk in His path to please Him, they know His promise that death is not the end of everything. Don't be afraid of death; there's life. This is the right way to go, the right thing to do.

Notes:

3 These verses in the Koran are found in Surah 3:48,49; 5:110; and Surah 6:36; 22:6. The numbering of verses varies in different translations of the Koran.

Hiding
the Dish

Farah

I work for the government in a medical laboratory. I do blood tests mostly and inspect graphs. For about a year-and-a-half, my head used to ache, and I had some kind of dizziness.

One afternoon I went by my sister's home. I noticed something had changed. They were so gracious when I walked through the door. Her family was really loving toward me. They paid more attention to me than before, and they had so much joy. So, I decided to sit down and tell her how I felt. She came over to me and placed her hand on my arm and simply said, "I'm praying for you." On another day I had a great spell of this sickness in my mother's home. My sister came to the house and sat quietly beside my bed. She began to pray. I was so sick in bed for thirteen days, but she stayed near me.

During this time, she placed a booklet in my hand. I sat up and saw the title: "Wonderful." I learned that this is one of the names of Jesus. As she placed some tea beside me, she asked, "While you're in bed, would you read this booklet?" Even with my headache, I nodded yes. "Read this carefully, and see what it's telling you." All my life I had been praying in the Muslim way, but I wasn't really a fanatic. I was just kind of trying to please Allah in a way, I mean, the Muslim god, but I felt some kind of emptiness in myself.

I asked Allah, "What can I do to fill myself up and completely take care of this emptiness?" That evening my husband saw the booklet on the table by my bed, but he didn't object to it. He said, "You go ahead and read it." I read it over and over. I had never seen anything like it. That same week my sister returned and gave me a New Testament. She said, "Read this book, and concentrate on it. It's going to fulfill you; that emptiness in you will be gone if you read this book completely." Still in bed, I read the book, a few pages at a time.

My bedroom had windows all around, so it was very light because of the sun outside. I would prop myself up and slowly turn the pages. One day it just started giving me peace, wonderful peace. I cannot really explain how I felt when I was reading this New Testament. Although I was the only one becoming a Christian in my family, my husband didn't say anything. He also likes to study. He has always encouraged me to read, to learn something. He began to see me with the Bible a lot, but he didn't say anything about it. He's very quiet.

Lately, I see that the Bible has moved around our bedroom some. It moves around from one table or another table or sometimes on the bed. But I didn't move it. My husband picks it up, but I don't pressure him. You know, it's very hard to push Iranian men into doing anything.

One day as I was reading this Bible, my husband said, "You never read anything, but you're really reading now; studying to learn something, aren't you?" I talk a lot with my husband, but when I was reading the book, I wasn't talking as much as I used to. My husband is saying, "What's happening here?" He never reads the Koran. But I notice that now the pages of the Bible are moved. It looks like he is reading a few pages a day these last eighteen months.

Now I tell my children to come read this book. Recently, I got two other Bibles, and I gave them to my teenage son and daughter. I declared, "I have one; let's read them together." My daughter is very smart. She is fifteen and reads the Bible every day. I'm getting her ready to know Jesus Christ.

Where I live in a little city, they're not really as fanatical as the people in the big city of Isfahan. There you have to run and hide any Christian book in different places before people walk in your home. Here in our town, in my husband's family, praying five times a day and all that kind of stuff doesn't exist.

I want to be a witness for Jesus Christ. I put two Bibles out just like the Muslims do the Koran. I purposely leave the books on my coffee table so when the people come in the door, they can see the Bible and literature spread there.

Sometimes they are curious and ask questions. I am ready to answer them.

In my office at the laboratory, there's a television broadcast every day with all Iranian religious material, the faces of the prophets, and mournful songs. I smile and tell our staff, "Let's turn it off, turn it off." I smile and walk over to turn it off. They become curious about me.

One afternoon after work, two of my coworkers from the lab came to my home. Like me as women, they must wear the black clothes, called a *chador*, but I knew they weren't really fanatic. When they saw the Bible on my coffee table, they turned and looked at me. One of them picked it up and asked, "What are you reading?" I replied, "I'm reading about the life of Jesus Christ." She carefully laid it back down and commented, "Oh, good." The other said, "Oh, you're going in the other way, aren't you?" I said, "Yeah, I don't want to bother with the other book. I'm just reading the Bible and learning more. It's truth that I'm looking for."

Many Iranians are tired of fanaticism and are against the regime. They are searching. Ten days before I traveled to a secret Christian meeting, I went to my sister-in-law's house and said, "I'm going to go to another city." My husband jumped up in the middle of our conversation and said, "Yeah, she's going to go become a Christian." They weren't angry, just curious. Iran is a nation of young people and very highly educated.

Whoever reads my story, whenever you get together, pray for us. Pray for Iran so we can be released from this chain of Islam. They give us a hard time really. My husband is a government employee, and because his salary is so little, we couldn't really have enough money to pay for our rent. I had to leave our children with my mother-in-law so I can find a part-time job to help our income. My husband's salary is only $50 a month. When I went to work, our income got better.

Back then my mind was so shattered, but now every time I start reading the Bible, it gives me peace and serenity. The city I live in is famous for unbelievers and unbelief. They believe in nothing. Sixty percent of these people are really free and nonchalant about the Koran and Islam or any religion.

> PRAY FOR US.
> PRAY FOR IRAN
> SO WE CAN BE
> RELEASED FROM
> THIS CHAIN
> OF ISLAM.

The two girls who came to my home are really open and ready to read. I'm going to give them the Bible. They don't like wearing this black clothing. These things that they ask us to wear look like we are in a prison. We are all in a prison actually. They want this dress to be from our heart, but it is not. It's so hot wearing this black under the sun, but we have to wear it. We suffer. This year they ease off a little bit, but in some places we still have to wear it. I've been wearing these jeans under it. I wear jeans and the *manteau* (overcoat) that goes half to three-quarters down. You can see our cloth pant leg now below our knee.

We watch some Christian singing and teaching from other countries with a satellite dish. Twice the police took our satellite dish off the roof of our condo and carried it away. One day the police drove up to our neighbor's house and climbed up on his roof. They just grabbed his satellite dish and brought it down. The neighbor warned me because he knew they might give us a problem. Our dish is covered with canvas to hide it. We made a sheet for it. We also took it down for a while because I'm also a government employee. If they find out that I have a TV satellite dish, they might cut my job. Some people put their dish on the balcony, but they still put a canvas sheet in front of it.

These Iranian Christian programs are beamed in at night. We get together with a few other women and close the door. One time I took both my children to a "satellite meeting." Our daughter came and started singing with us, but my son sat around the corner in the hallway. He was kind of bashful since the majority there were women. I told him when he was sitting back there to be sure to listen to what we're doing and what we're saying.

I was baptized in a tub in a house. I hope those reading this will follow Jesus' way. It is full of grace and blessing. Pray for my husband as he is learning from watching me. I wish I could have received Jesus twelve years ago.

The
FANATIC

&

Jilla

In the sixth grade, I became a *baseige*—a girl who is dedicated to Islam, completely involved, almost like a military-style worship. In school I would take the microphone and sing mournfully like in a funeral service, almost as if the prophet Hussein (Mohammed's grandson) had just died, although he died thousands of years ago. Then we hit ourselves. Because I had the microphone in one hand, I would hit myself harder than everybody else and would bleed. In school they taught me that whoever would fast the longest would have a more secure place in heaven. I did that for such a long time that once I ended up in the hospital.

We wore a special card with our picture on it like a badge. To wear the card, we had to have memorized the entire Koran and pass other tests. We used a safety pin to pin it on our clothing. We also had an armband and had to

Women of the basiege *who have memorized the Koran*

wear a cap to cover our hair. They gave us a little band to tie on our hair whenever we went out from among the women. These had phrases in Arabic on them such as, "We are the troops of Fatima al Zahra" (the wife of Mohammed).

We were flooded with all kinds of spiritual laws. Because I was the baseige leader for three years, the girls at school would all look to me to lead them in prayer. Everybody had to pray, especially during the month of Hussein.

The Muslim prophet Hussein's grave is in Iraq. We remember his martyrdom around October. Every year at this time a dark spirit would come over me. Under Islam I was always grieving. We have three months when we grieve for Hussein. When I would feel like this, my peace would leave. I thought this was my fault because I'm such a horrible sinner.

I would parade in the street with the others, walking without any shoes until it was very painful. This was a ritual performed for cleansing.

As ninth graders, we would pitch a tent on the school grounds. Men would come with sticks bearing chains and beat themselves on their backs during worship. They would bring things like tambourines and drums to make them focus while they flogged their bodies. We women would hit ourselves with only our hands because we didn't have the sticks. We thought we should hit ourselves very hard, also our head. Perhaps half of my headaches were from those days. These fanatic groups still exist today.

Back when I was in the first grade, I always wanted more of Allah. I asked my mom and dad if I could learn how to pray the prayers. I would lay out my white prayer cloth on the floor, place another cloth on top, and then lay a handkerchief with a stone on top. The stone was a tablet of compressed dirt from Mecca. They call it a stamp. We have to put our nose on the stone. Some people eat it actually, little by little, because they feel that it's good for anemia, and they also feel that it's holy. After I would finish praying, I would pick up this stone and the white, decorated material, and right underneath it would be money. I thought the Allah I was praying to had put the money there, but I didn't want the money. I wanted the Truth.

Other people's love couldn't get my complete attention or affection, even my mother and father's love. I didn't build close relationships very quickly, and even until now, I've never had a boyfriend. Some people in Iran from the time they're very young, fill their heart with other things. I wanted more of Allah.

Until I was eighteen, I really felt Allah had put that money under my prayer cloth, but then I learned that my parents were doing this. I would pray five different times from early morning until late at night. I would bow 400 times in four different directions. When I woke up in the morning, my knees would hurt.

I WOULD PRAY FIVE TIMES FROM EARLY MORNING UNTIL LATE AT NIGHT. I WOULD BOW 400 TIMES IN FOUR DIRECTIONS.

After each prayer event, I would take the cloths back to the special drawers in my dresser because the cloths are kept very, very clean. I would place my Koran there as well as another book that I used.

My four sisters and one brother all kept their prayer cloths in these drawers, but they didn't use them. They would take them out once a year at the Muslim time of Ramadan, the month when you're supposed to pray and fast. I would take my little brother by his hand, kneel down, and show him how to pray. My father used to pray, during the Iran-Iraq war and during the Islamic revolution. But when all the religious sects came into authority forcing us to worship, he was hurt by that and stopped praying.

My uncle has a bruise on his forehead from hitting the floor during his prayers. He's done it so much he made a scar. Many men have this scar or bump as a sign of their holiness. But the men in my immediate family never read the Koran. In my search for more, I would read three verses of the Koran a day with my prayers, then begin to memorize them. Still this did not satisfy me, so I went and got another religious book, *How to Be Connected with Allah*, a book of older written prayers. This Islamic book, like many, is written in Arabic, not our national language of Farsi.

We are taught Arabic in school and told that only the Arabic language can best reveal Allah, not our own native language. Learning these prayers in Arabic from such a young age, I kept adding more and more prayers, seeking after Allah. Sometimes even the mullahs didn't do that many prayers.

On the days when I had an examination but could hear the prayers from the mosques through a window, I would pause and pray with them. I went to the mosque every Friday. On the days that I couldn't go, I would pray wherever I was.

In the mosque I had to stand behind a huge curtain in the middle, dividing the men from the women. The women are all behind the black curtain. First, we stand up, and a person in front up high begins to say prayers. The women can only hear the mullah's voice from the microphone, but we cannot see him. We can only listen and repeat the prayers aloud, kneeling on the carpet while bowing over and over.

Many of the women needing spiritual or emotional help make an appointment with the mullah for counseling.

He sees them and wants them sexually, calling them "temporary wives," so women very rarely see him.

One of the Imams told everyone throughout the entire Middle East, "I want women to be able to come and see me when I am doing these wonderful prayers. I am going to take a large number of temporary wives, and they will represent all women. They can come in and see me." Then he sleeps with them. It's horrible how they have this religious thing where you can be joined in a "marriage of convenience" for only five days, sometimes signing marriage and divorce documents as you go in and out.

It's supposed to be very spiritualized and is not called prostitution. The women do it thinking they'll have a child and the child will be holy, then Allah will look favorably on them. This happens throughout the Middle East. But Arabic men mostly use this practice. Even in non-Arabic Iran, the Arabic men are the ones who do this the most.

Even with my religious zeal, I knew these things were wrong and continued to search for goodness. One time my two sisters and I went to see a play in a large city. Curious, we visited a church where tourists frequent, but they wouldn't let us in. So we went to a small side room because we felt drawn to this place. It was very tiny.

An old man sitting there at a table was selling candles to people. We walked over, bought some candles and lit them. When I placed my candle at the front, I said, "Lord, God, I want to find You."

My sisters walked off somewhere else, but I was drawn to another room. It was very bright. I went in there and saw how the room had a nice feeling, almost a spiritual thing. I sat on a little tiny bench on one side then looked up. There was a huge picture of Jesus in front of me. Something just made me fall to my knees. I began to cry very heavily.

My sisters came back into the room, which had a dirt floor. They saw me kneeling and said, "Get up, get up, you're going to get all dirty." They wiped the dust off my black robe. We left the building and went home.

Before my salvation, I was in Isfahan one time in a great big square where they sell things. I saw a jewelry cross from very far away, the kind worn by Armenians. I went toward it. Although it was made of an inferior metal, I bought it and put it on and wore it all the time. It would never turn black or anything. I decided to buy a longer chain for it and made sure it stayed outside of my clothing so people would see it. But wearing it did not bring me peace.

At age nineteen, I needed spiritual and physical relief but did not know where to go. I would get migraine headaches so bad I would hit my head on the wall hoping to relieve the pain. I would take medicine for it, but nothing would work. I would pull my hair down really hard, pressing my hands on my head, trying to stop something that felt like swelling. It was so horrible that we thought I had cancer or something.

Later, my family took me to the Muslim prayer writer. He is almost like a fortuneteller. He prophesied I wouldn't live more than two years. As we paid him, he started writing me several prayers stating, "I can only help you live just a little bit longer." He gave me some holy water to splash around our house and some incense to burn in our rooms. My mother would take a long tub and put the paper slips of his prayers into the tub. Then she would pour water over the prayers to make more holy water. Some had phrases from the Koran written on them. We would splash the water around the rooms and anoint the different areas of our home.

My father worked in a large factory carrying heavy material. His knees got ruined and were very painful so he became addicted to drugs. I would take the wet paper prayers out of the tub, squeeze them out, and my mother would put them in my father's pockets hoping he would be healed from his addiction.

I WASHED CARPETS FROM MORNING TILL NIGHT. I THOUGHT THIS WOULD GET ME TO HEAVEN.

By now I used Muslim beads to pray so I would not forget the order of the prayers. I would wear them around my neck during the day. But I had heard that when you die, you wouldn't have any beads with you. So you have to learn to count the prayers by tapping the joints of your hands. I did this so many times my hands were always sore.

There was a small room for prayer in our neighborhood just for women. We would go in there and go around and around bowing in prayer. There was another large house someone had dedicated to the name of the Muslim prophet Hussein. The whole first floor was full of carpets. I wanted God in my life so badly I thought, "I'll dedicate myself to wash all of those carpets." They are normally washed once a year, but I washed carpets from morning till night. When I went to bed at night, my hands were so swollen I had to have them wrapped up in cloths. I thought this would get me to heaven.

For a few years, I was a religious actress in the international theater. Once we went to an international conference, a dramatic workshop, and some people were there from Armenia. An Armenian woman walked over and asked me for some hair clips. I remembered this woman and their play, which was about freedom. I told her, "I liked that play very much. Can I have your autograph?" The Armenians allowed me to participate in their play.

One part was about many gods. My line was, "Which one is our God?" In the dialog they named many of their Greek gods. In the play we would repeat, "So which one is our God?" But we would never answer that. Instead we would say, "We want the God who is the God of truth and light, the one who has the bow and arrow." At the climax of the play, they showed a resurrection.

In the next play, I played the role of Sanam, who was a lover. This person Sanam is in love and is very free. On the stage I would ride a bicycle going around and looking up to the sky. My lines were: "Who am I? What am I doing here? What am I supposed to do?" When I would say these words out loud, I would say privately to myself, *Really—why am I here?* As I rode around the stage, this question would go deep into my heart.

129

During this time of my life, one of my sisters came back from college to our small town and brought a movie with her. It was the life of Christ according to Luke. I went to a room of our house and sat on the carpet where we all watch TV. I just happened to be alone and put the movie in. While watching how Jesus loved people, I began to cry. At the end of the film, there was the prayer of repentance. I prayed it six times. I rewound the tape to the prayer, backwards, forwards, backwards and forwards. I don't think I realized what repentance meant, but I wanted to be near to God.

I automatically went on my knees and started lifting up my hands. I was always jealous of my sister after she came back from college because she would kneel down and without any Muslim beads or clothes or holy stones, she would lift up her hands and start praying.

Still alone, I kept praying, saying, "God, I want to have that connection, that feeling that I see my sister has." I would cry and pray and ask God over and over. By that time everyone came home.

I thought, *Well, this is it. This is what I am looking for.* I began to pray in Farsi that I would be delivered from sin. It was like God was talking to me, through me. He was saying, "This is the truth. I am the true God. I am the one God." I ran into the kitchen and found my saved sister. I just had to tell her.

My sister, so surprised, just threw her hands up and said, "I don't know what to tell you. I don't have any teaching yet."

I felt so lonely. So I went into the room again where I had been on my knees. Frustrated, I started hitting myself on my chest in the Islamic way. I didn't know what to do next, so I watched the film again.

I didn't tell my friends about Jesus those first few days. I always told them everything. I was not afraid. I began to have much peace, and my headaches were cured.

Later my father, who was very protective, allowed my sister and me to move to the city. The two of us rented a room. This had to be God's plan. Now together, we were free to talk about Jesus.

My sister had gone to the university in Tehran. There she had heard of a church where we could find some Christians. A few churches are permitted in Iran for the small Armenian minority. We tried to find a church.

A family in our neighborhood was watching over us in our apartment, watching everywhere we went and asking everything we did. When we left our apartment one morning, they didn't know our intentions. We found the church and quickly turned in at the entrance. No one stopped us at the door. Rows of men and women were singing. We found a seat in the back and sat down, watching intently. Most were Armenian non-Muslims. As a demonstration of religious freedom, the government allows their church.

During the singing and while the sermon was going on, I kept feeling something poured over my head. After the service, they said, "Anybody who wants to pray, come to the prayer room in the back." I went with my sister to the prayer room. When an elder prayed, I felt pain coming out, leaving me. A lady walked up to me and said, "Have you repented?" I said, "What's that?" She told me the meaning of repentance, and then I began to pray.

My sister, who had given me the film about Jesus, was so amazed at what was happening with me. Here I was, crying and praying loudly. We left the service and made our way back home discussing the morning. This was our first time to be with Christians.

Back in our small apartment room, we didn't have any furniture. It was a bare place. There were our sleeping mats and a stack of our folded clothing. I didn't have my own Bible yet. All I had was a colored picture of Jesus about six inches tall with a frame painted with flowers. He was looking to one side. To feel close to Him, I would pull my sleeping mat over and sit on the side He was looking at.

Sitting over in my selected corner of the room, I felt His eyes were always looking at me because they were looking in this one direction. I felt He was fathering me and loving me through that picture.

Later, the Christians led us to a home group of five or six Christians who had left Islam. Our names are Muslim, not Armenian. The authorities do not like us to attend a church, and culturally we are somewhat different. So the home group was good for our physical and spiritual security. We had been really touched by Christ. In the big church where many people walk in, you could see everything. Some of the people who came weren't really changed by Christ. The girls would come just to find husbands, so they would dress very badly, wearing tight clothes and showing too much skin. We were embarrassed and not ready to see this.

In the home group, it was much more intimate, and we received teaching. The focus of staying pure made me feel more sensitive. Before I was a Christian, I was very controlling. I had ideas of being something like a queen on high or somebody who had authority so I could tell the people how to do things right and wrong. But after knowing Christ, I wanted to be with people where they are. I wanted to be an ambassador and deliver the message of Christ to them.

At first we just focused on the New Testament. Sharing one, we huddled together. As time went by and I grew, and they began to give me more books, I read books like *The Life and Resurrection, The Alpha and Omega*, and others.

After a time of preaching from our leader, he gave us Bible courses from the church. He would take the studies and divide them up and give them to each person. Some studies we would complete ourselves and then review them with him. When we got to the more difficult things like "the righteousness of God," and things like that, we worked with him. The pastor had a little library. He would loan books to us. This was a very dangerous act.

Finally, I got my own New Testament from my group leader. I was so happy. In Iran, Christians or curious Muslims must travel hundreds of miles to find one. The Bible Society was closed after 1979, when we became an Islamic Republic.

Our Bible study group still meets in the same place today, in a very poor home; the walls are made of mud. There's a door at the alleyway, and you go way up a very tight stairway to their apartment. It is very simple, but from all the walls, love radiates.

A few months later, our family joined us in the city, so my sister and I gave up our apartment. My parents see the joy and peace we have and permit us to meet with Christians in our family apartment. We pray every day an hour before the meeting that all the eyes and ears of the neighbors would be closed so the people can come in whenever they want. The family members from both my mother's and father's side are very fanatical Muslims, and they still watch us all the time, trying to catch us. We have many sessions in our home every week, but we just pray, and God closes their eyes.

To protect our family when we all moved in together, I felt it wouldn't be right to keep the picture of Jesus. This would endanger everyone, so we took down all the Christian pictures. Muslim family members from my mom's or dad's family also visit us. If a Christian friend of ours walks in, we say, "This is my Father's friend." I am not lying. My God is also my Father, and Christians are also my family.

Many women Muslim converts are beaten, especially those from our little home church groups. The boys are also beaten for their Christianity. Their own family sometimes does this, and the family won't speak to them. One of my friends is a boy who had spent three years in an Islamic school. His parents had little or nothing to do with him during those three years. He was so sad. But when he received Christ, he came home. He was changed and happy and strong. Now they're rejecting him and beating him up, but he still attends our home group.

Sometimes when we get together, we will hear testimonies like, "This week this bad thing happened to me, but I still hide my Bible and went to another place and read it secretly." One boy will go sit in his family car at night lying down on the seat and read the Scripture with a flashlight.

> WE'RE ALL LEARNING TO UNDERSTAND HOW THE APOSTLE PAUL HAD TO SUFFER THINGS AND WHAT THIS FELT LIKE.
>
> ❦❧

We're all learning to understand how the apostle Paul had to suffer things and what this felt like. When our Christian friends tell us these things happen, we want to share the pain with them. We read about Paul together and pray with them. If we feel it's going to be really dangerous, we start fasting.

The girls are under a lot more pressure than the boys. Sometimes they will miss a meeting, so we have a system set up of talking in code on the phone. We always talk by code with this person to learn what happened to them. Some of our code words even use Muslim terms or sports terms and so on.

When I first came to Christ, although I had visited the church only two or three times, I couldn't wait to share Jesus with others. Within six weeks of seeing the film about Jesus, I started sharing on the bus. I really came to a greater faith studying Scripture after that, and I left the university to have more time for Bible study.

I worked in a day care and then got a job at a company as a janitor. I cleaned, served tea and cookies, and did typing. I took my Bible with me every day. In the morning I would go in much earlier before we started and have my devotions. When the engineers would gather in a conference room for meetings and didn't need me, I would sit down really quickly and use these extra minutes to read.

> *T*HESE PEOPLE IN IRAN ARE IN THE SAME SORT OF PRISON THAT I WAS IN. I MUST SHARE WITH THEM WHAT RELEASED ME.

In the morning on the bus ride to work, I would witness to two or three people and again in the evening on my way home. In the middle of the bus is a big, long rail that divides the men's and women's areas. I would be on one side witnessing to a woman, but the men across the rail would also be listening. They would be very interested.

As we moved this way through the streets, I always carried two things: a Bible and the Jesus movie because some of the women couldn't read. I would try to find out if they could read. If they couldn't read, I would give them the movie. I usually wouldn't give anything to people directly until I had met with them and talked with them several times while commuting. Sometimes I could just whip something out of my pocket real quick and give it to them saying, "This is mine, but I'll let you have it." They would slide it inside their bag or their clothing.

God has given me discernment for the character of people and their pain. Sometimes I'll see a woman sitting, looking very depressed and staring out the window. All of a sudden, I'll say, "Isn't God wonderful, isn't He beautiful, doesn't He just make you full of joy?" Then the woman will turn around and look at me like, "What's the matter with you?" Or they will be having an ice cream cone, and I'll say, "It's delicious, huh?" And they'll say, "Yeah." And I'll say, "You know, salvation is even more delicious than that." It was amazing how quickly they would give me their phone number.

Although I went to a church, they never said anything about sharing your faith. Perhaps they are afraid of the government. But even in the house group at the very beginning, they are cautious and don't say anything about sharing your faith. But at one point, I realized I've been freed of so many things, and these people in Iran are in the same sort of prison that I was in. I must share with them what released me. I was sorry for these poor people. Later, I would disciple these converts from the bus. I would start from Genesis and go all the way to the cross.

One evening there was a young woman sitting beside me. The bus was very crowded going back home because this is when everybody is getting off work. I had taught myself to pray and intercede for the person sitting beside me and also for the driver and everybody else getting off and on at the stops. But I was so tired as I was returning home this particular day.

I ended up sleeping on this lady's shoulder, not saying anything to her, but falling asleep in prayer. When the bus got to the very last stop, the lady woke me up and said, "You know, it's the last stop." I said, "Okay." So we got off the bus together. It was also my stop.

The next day on the bus, I turned around and saw we were standing again side by side. She was smiling at me. She said, "Do you want to sleep on my shoulder today?" I replied, "Did I sleep on your shoulder yesterday?" She said, "Yes, and as a matter of fact, I got a lot of peace from you." I smiled, "That's because God gives me that peace."

As we held on turning corners in the traffic, I started from the beginning telling her about God. She began telling me about her need and her pain. I found out that yesterday she had wanted to kill herself.

"As a matter of fact," she said, "I can't lie. I was so frustrated with life. When you fell asleep on my shoulder, I just wanted to push you and make you fall down. But when you were asleep on my shoulder, I felt something like love come into my body." She said, "I prayed, 'God, I hope I see her again tomorrow because I don't have the courage to talk to her today.'" I encouraged her, "Be assured that if my head was on your shoulder and you felt that, it was from God."

She was in such a weak emotional condition I felt it was best for two weeks that I make her "thirsty" with small sips of God's love. For two weeks, this lady kept saying,

"Hey, I want to repent. I want to receive Christ." I would say, "No, wait." After two weeks, I told her the whole gospel. We went to each other's homes, and I taught her the Word of God. She was only a year or two older than me, and she didn't have a husband. Finally, I gave her a New Testament, and then after a long time, I gave her the film.

We can always face suffering for our witness. In a city north of Tehran, some people in a home group had been persecuted, so all the Christians who knew each other started going around saying, "Don't witness." I was thinking, "God, You know something's not right. What do You want me to do here?"

The message continued to spread by mouth among the different Christians, "You must stop witnessing right now because there's a lot of persecution." I started praying, "God, so what are we supposed to do to obey You?" We began a time of intercession, not witnessing yet. We walked on the hills above other cities and through the streets praying silently for the people. This is how we started going to different cities to witness even more. So the persecution had pushed us out to new areas.

In Iran, the people are so snoopy, looking at us as soon as just a few people sit down somewhere together, especially young people. One time we went to the park with families and children. There we don't look so weird and are able to gather without being investigated. When we see each other on the street, we can't even talk to each other or stand by each other. But in the house church, inside a meeting, we're free to trade notes and talk. We trade with each other

Christian tracts we find, as well as books, songs, and CDs with Scripture and Christian teaching on them.

Some of us have computers, so we started witnessing on the Internet. This has given us a lot of fruit. When we see that people have really truly repented on the Internet, we stay in touch with them for about a month. Then we ask for their name and phone number, and we go visit them. A lot of the people who are in the worst persecution are actually the ones who are saved through the Internet, because they're usually the only one in the family. If I know I'm making a trip to share Christ, I get on the Internet the weeks before that and start trying to find young people from that area.

In Iran, there are chat rooms just for the people from their areas. The authorities trace e-mails, but not chats. They also track text messaging, trying to find us.

I witnessed one time to people in India; three of them wanted to receive the Lord. I also shared with some in England. We send them Scriptures and try to find the Scriptures in English. This was very difficult because I don't know any English at all. So we finally gave up on that.

Today I love to clean house churches. I've been doing that since a week after I was born-again. I was so happy to do this because I'd asked God for a ministry. And I wanted myself to be changed. In Islam I had done that, so now, all the more. It's so interesting to see the reaction of people. They thought I was just looking for praise. But when they saw my joy, a singing, happy soul as I was sweeping or washing, they allowed me to do it.

The Fanatic

I began a ministry with girls who were living un-
healthy lives. I was in a taxi one day and saw a woman who
was dressed very suggestively. I began to share with her
how God had changed my life. She said, "Well, you know,
whatever. But I'd like to hear more another time. I've got
to go." We exchanged phone numbers. That night when I
went to sleep, I saw a dream of the life of this lady. So I
called the lady and said, "Excuse me, but I had this dream
about you." I told her the dream, and the lady was really
shocked because it was about her.

In the dream I saw she was pregnant. I asked, "Are you
pregnant? I saw a dream." And she replied, "Yes, I am. How
did you know that?" This lady who's pregnant had a neighbor who owns a beauty salon who was also doing wrong
things. One night this neighbor saw a dream of Jesus. She
saw Jesus come to her salon and open the cash drawer to
take something valuable and start distributing it to people...like seeds. So the other lady who's pregnant told her,
"I know somebody who knows Jesus. She can help you..."
So they called me.

We arranged to meet in the beauty salon. As we were
visiting, a woman dressed in a chador, the kind very fanatical religious women wear, came in and sat down. Her black
chador, which covered her clothing, was drawn even more
tightly around her head and face. It was more perfect-
looking than ours. Suddenly she began talking very badly,
telling very nasty jokes. Then, since we were all women
and inside a building, she took her chador off and sat down,
talking badly again. I was sitting there thinking, *How can*

this person who is supposed to be so dedicated to Islam talk so badly? I sat there in a corner quietly praying in my heart. All of a sudden the woman stopped and turned to me exclaiming, "My, you're so full of light!"

I had not said a word yet. Then the woman raised her palm upward and gave an Islamic statement, "Blessed are those who know much about Allah." This is an honorable saying for those of high faith. I replied to her, "Our Allah [God] is a God who's for everyone." With a curious look, the lady declared, "Keep talking. I want to hear more of what you have to say."

I had prayed before going there that no one would come in the shop to stop us. No one else walked in. We were not having our hair done. The woman who owned the shop seemed inspired. "What should I do to make this place kind of like, holy?" I said, "Well, you should take these seeing eyes off your wall."

The Islamic prayer writers, who are like sub-mullahs, write scriptures from the Koran and stick them to one of the two eyes, the seeing eyes. Muslims place these on their walls hoping for blessing or luck, or to keep away evil. These were stuck on the walls of the beauty shop—the eyes staring down at us. Sometimes they represent an "evil eye."

I just got up and started grabbing these Koran scriptures and the eyes off of the walls where they had stuck them. I put them away then started talking about Jesus and God. I spoke to them about the love of God. "You all have a need for the love of God. This is why you are in these situations."

Then I took my Bible and started praying, walking to all four corners of the room. The others sat watching me. The outwardly religious Muslim woman said in a surprised voice, "Jesus has come here."

The second time I went to the shop, the little group was waiting for me. We started studying about sin. A prostitute walked in as we sat together. I just continued. Hearing our conversation, she leaned over and told me about her drug addiction. I told her about the peace of God.

Then another customer walked in and sat in the chair to have her hair done. But listening to us, she turned and said, "I'm very sick." I had learned to pray through the Scriptures. While doing that, I read that Jesus was the healer. I said, "Can I pray for you to be healed?" She agreed, so I prayed for her that God would touch her. As we began to talk again about sin, another woman came, but this time from upstairs, above the shop. The shop lady was doing hair and didn't have time to help her. So she sat down beside her to wait. We stopped our study and talked to her, and within a few minutes, she gladly received Christ. She was very ready.

ALL OF A SUDDEN THE WOMAN STOPPED AND TURNED TO ME EXCLAIMING, "MY, YOU'RE SO FULL OF LIGHT!"

We learned later that the one who had been pregnant had a miscarriage. She had just received Christ. Her boyfriend returned to her and said, "Okay, I want to marry you." She came to me and said, "What should I do?" I said,

"Does he know Christ? Of course he doesn't know Christ. No, it's not in God's will. Tell him, 'No.'" I had been studying with her less than a month. Even so, she courageously told her boyfriend, "No, I don't want to marry you."

Now I have dedicated my Mondays to going to that shop. I got a report later from the woman, "From the day you cleaned my shop, I used to have two or three customers a week, and now I can't even keep up with all the business coming to it, it's so blessed." The lady's business has been so successful that now she just closes the whole shop on Mondays.

> *I* ALWAYS TAKE PEOPLE WHO ARE NOT WITNESSING TO TEACH THEM HOW TO BE BOLD FOR JESUS AND TO EXPERIENCE THE JOY OF WINNING SOULS.

I go regularly to six or seven cities and recently began to visit three more new cities. I pray first and ask God, "Who do You want me to take?" Then I pray for the person who goes with me. I always take people who are not witnessing to teach them how to be bold for Jesus and to experience the joy of winning souls. We have a very low budget for evangelistic trips.

Sometimes we leave on the bus at 11:00 at night and arrive in the afternoon. We stay overnight, then start back home at 6:00 p.m., arriving home early morning in time to go to work.

During an evangelistic trip, we minister strictly in the street. First, we pray over the city for a while then we go into the city and walk. We go into shops to blend in. Inside the shops seems to be a very fruitful place for us to witness. I carry a big bag full of videos, CDs, books, and Bibles. I also take a lot of little tracts called "The Most Important Decision in Your Life."

In one city we began a growing house group of more than twenty-five. These are usually people who are addicts and have lives like that. It's so bad. Even if you stand near them in public, you can tell what they're into. We lay hands on them, and unbelievable things come out of them. Every Saturday while we are on these trips, we fast.

I am twenty years old and have been a Christian two years. I must serve Jesus. I read in the Bible how we are the Body of Christ, the hands and feet of Jesus. I feel I'm only the little toe of Jesus. I feel like we all should have unity together if we just can see it. In Christ we are one Body. But when we experience that one leg of the church is here and one hand is over there and one piece is over here, then no one can be effective. It's as if you have a hand, and the whole hand wants to grow, but the little finger stays this small. Isn't that ugly?

My favorite Bible verse is John 3:16: "For God so loved the world that He gave His one and only Son, that whoever believes in Him shall not perish but have eternal life." I was thinking, "Lord, I don't want to waste my time, even in sharing my testimony. I hope my story will not shrink to nothing at one point. Let every word be something that becomes like a mountain of strength to someone."

I always wanted to get to Christ with my own efforts. But when I finally got to the point where I was so broken, that's when Jesus came to me. I don't think I was the one who was trying to get to Him at all. I didn't do anything to get to Him. I would leave you with Revelation 3:20. Ask Him to come into your heart. You will sup with Him, and He will sup with you.

Editor's Note: Doctors report that the little toe is essential for a balanced walk.

HELP TO IRANIAN CHRISTIANS

∽∾

The Voice of the Martyrs provides evangelistic tools for our brothers and sisters in Iran, supporting efforts such as:

- Christian television broadcasts
- Distribution of the *JESUS* Film
- Printing of Bibles and Christian literature

To learn more about VOM's work in Iran and how you can be involved, contact the VOM office nearest you (see the list on pages 151–152).

RESOURCES

Other Recommended Titles by The Voice of the Martyrs

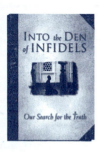

Into the Den of Infidels

Read the compelling stories of eight Muslims in Egypt—the intellectual capital of Islam—as they persevered until they discovered the truth.

To counteract Christian evangelism, a Muslim zealot set out to expose the false teachings in the Torah and the Bible. Instead, he found the true faith in Jesus, who changed him: "He did what the God of Mohammed was unable to do."

Raised to hate Christians, never imagining that they could be right, Mozafar discovered something that shook his whole being. After years of intense research, he had no choice but to face the truth—whatever the cost...

After years of railing against God, Khalil was caught by a love that wouldn't let him go. He cried out to God to know the truth: Who is this person anticipated by all nations, by Jews, Christians and Muslims? Unable to bear the struggle any longer, he gave his heart to the One who filled his inner being with joy...

In their own words, read these accounts and more, of Muslims in Egypt who found Christ.

Hearts of Fire

Eight women from eight very different backgrounds, yet the struggles they each faced rang with eerie similarity. From Pakistan, India, Romania, the former Soviet Union, China, Vietnam, Nepal, and Indonesia, these women shared similar experiences of hardship and persecution—all for their faith in Christ—yet they have emerged from adversity as leaders and heroines.

Wear the Crown
(Book and DVD Set)

Change the way you view your life in light of the persecuted church worldwide! Across the globe our brothers and sisters are suffering for Christ, yet they will not deny Him.

The *Wear the Crown* book features powerful full-color photographs and courageous stories of these ordinary men and women who find extraordinary strength in their complete surrender to the Lord. The "Wear the Crown" DVD is a high-impact music video featuring Christian artist Bill Drake. Introduce your friends or church to this powerful visual tool.

This book and DVD set will motivate you to eagerly seek this same depth of relationship with Christ and includes ways to encourage our persecuted family and grow in your personal faith.

The Voice of the Martyrs has available many other books, videos, brochures, and other products to help you learn more about the persecuted church. To order materials, or receive our free monthly newsletter, call or write:

The Voice of the Martyrs
P. O. Box 443
Bartlesville, OK 74005-0443
Phone: 800-747-0085
Website: www.persecution.com

The Voice of the Martyrs
P.O. Box 117
Port Credit
Mississauga ON L5G 4L5
Canada
Phone: 1-905-670-9721
Website: www.persecution.net

The Voice of the Martyrs
P.O. Box 250
Lawson NSW 2783
Australia
Phone: 02 4759 3700
Website: www.persecution.com.au

Christian Mission International
P.O. Box 7157
1417 Primrose Hill
South Africa
Phone: 011-873-2604

Release International
P.O. Box 54
Orpington BR5 9RT
United Kingdom
Phone: 44 (0) 1689 823491
Website: www.releaseinternational.org

Voice of the Martyrs
P.O. Box 5482
Papanui
Christchurch 8005
New Zealand
Phone: 64-9-837-1589
Website: www.persecution.co.nz